The Latino Journey to
Financial Greatness

The

Latino Journey

to Financial

Greatness

10 Steps to Creating Wealth,
Security, and a Prosperous Future for
You and Your Family

Louis Barajas

 rayo *An Imprint of* HarperCollins*Publishers*

HarperCollins books may be purchased for educational, business, or sales
promotional use. For information, please write: Special Markets Department,
HarperCollins Publishers Inc., 10 East 53rd Street, New York, NY 10022.

FIRST EDITION

Printed on acid-free paper

Library of Congress Cataloging-in-Publication Data
Barajas, Louis
    The Latino journey to financial greatness : 10 steps to creating wealth,
security, and a prosperous future for you and your family / Louis Barajas.—
1st. ed.
        p. cm.
    ISBN 0-06-621422-X
    1. Hispanic Americans—Finance, Personal.   I. Title.
HG179 .296 2003
332.024'0368073—dc21   2002027592

03 04 05 06 07 WBC/RRD 10 9 8 7 6 5 4 3 2 1

To my grandmother, Socorro Medina.

I hope you are seeing from heaven how your unconditional love

is inspiring me to follow a journey to greatness.

Acknowledgments

My greatest inspiration is, and continues to be, my family. Dad, thank you for teaching me what hard work and passion can create. Mom, thank you for showing me to be humble among all things and to be grateful for all I have. Alexa, Aubrey, and Eddie, thank you for keeping my life balanced and feeling young every day. Bill, thank you for believing in my vision and having the courage to take a leap of faith and join the journey. Aaron, thank you for always being there when I have needed you to step in. Your loyalty is deeply appreciated. To my staff, thank you for believing in your education and not losing sight of how much you are needed in your community. To my clients, thank you for believing in my dream of creating financial greatness in our community. To my mentors, thank you for all your wisdom and guidance. To my wife, Angie, thank you for believing in my dream. Your daily support and love make all the difference in the world.

I also want to thank several people who have made this book possible. It all started over 11 years ago when I met a gentleman named Phillip Rangel. Phillip entered my office in Boyle Heights in March 1992. He had read a column that George Ramos from the *Los Angeles Times* wrote about me. The article, which appeared on the front page of the Metro Section, described my move from Newport Beach back to East Los Angeles to open a financial planning business in the barrio. With nothing more than the newspaper and an idea of where my office was, Phillip showed up with a big smile and told me that he wanted to hire me as his financial planner. Phillip was born and raised in East Los Angeles but now lives in San Diego with his wife and children. At the time Phillip's wife, Carolyn, was executive assistant to Anthony Robbins, the motivational giant. Carolyn helped me attend Tony's Life Mastery Seminar in Maui.

At the seminar I met and roomed with David Bach. Meeting David was a blessed event. Even though David is younger than I am, he had already accomplished a lot. David and I came from totally different worlds, but it seemed that we shared similar dreams and goals. He published his first book, *Smart Women Finish Rich*, in 1999, and he has been my mentor throughout this project. David also introduced me to Victoria St. George, who masterfully helped edit this book. (Even though she doesn't speak a word of Spanish, Vicki manages to get inside my head and almost read my thoughts.) Through David, I also met Jan Miller, my literary agent. Jan and her assistant, Shannon Miser Marvin, worked extremely diligently to get my book published. Jan and Shannon make miracles happen in their office every day. In addition, I want to thank René Alegría of HarperCollins for believing in this project. His enthusiasm and expertise have made the process of publishing my first book effortless.

Finally, I want to thank God for putting all these people together in my life. I firmly believe that meeting them was no coincidence. After all, as someone once told me, coincidences are nothing more than God not taking the credit for his handiwork.

Contents

Part Three

Introduction

am the son of Mexican immigrants, and I grew up in the barrio of East Los Angeles. My father's story is typical of many
Latinos: He came to the United States at age 18, worked in a
factory during the day, and had a second job making and
installing lamps in the evenings and on weekends. After 17 years,
he used the income from his second job to start a small wrought-
iron business, which he owns to this day.

My father instilled in his children a belief in themselves and
their abilities. Like many first-generation Latinos, I did very well.
After getting my bachelor's degree in sociology at UCLA and
then receiving my MBA from the Claremont Graduate School of
Business, I worked for a couple of years at American Express as a
financial planner in Pasadena, California. Then I moved to Kenneth Leventhal, a prestigious accounting and consulting firm
based in the very upscale community of Newport Beach, California. I had an office overlooking the beach; I advised millionaire

clients; and I worked on several high-profile consulting projects. It was great—but it wasn't what I wanted. After a very short while, I realized that what I really wanted was to make a difference in the community I had come from. I believed the people in the barrio needed financial planning a lot more than my wealthy clients.

Two unfortunate events caused me to move much sooner than I expected. My grandmother, Socorro Medina, one of the few true loves of my life, passed away unexpectedly, and my uncle, Frank Medina, committed suicide shortly thereafter. My uncle was financially successful, but his wealth didn't make him happy. Naively, I had always thought money and success would make anyone very happy indeed. I found out the hard way, through my uncle and some of my wealthy clients, that this wasn't the case. Distraught, I sought spiritual advice from many different sources. Then one day a pastor told me that with all his years in the ministry and the hundreds of funerals he had attended, he had never seen a U-Haul behind a hearse. That did it. With the pastor's quote in mind, I gave my notice at Kenneth Leventhal, and in October 1991 I opened a financial planning firm in East Los Angeles.

For a while I got a lot of great press—"local kid makes good and returns home to give back." It was flattering, but all I really wanted to do was give my clients perspective. I wanted to show them how to reach financial freedom and still enjoy all the great values that Latinos espouse. I wanted them to achieve financial success without losing sight of the big picture. I wanted *financial greatness* for myself and my community.

Now, I didn't expect people to flock to my door, but I also didn't expect the kind of resistance I ran into when I told my neighbors in the barrio about my services. I was confused. After all, I knew these people and they knew me. I was one of their own, a Latino from the neighborhood—why wouldn't they trust me? And the ones who did come in, why were so many of them unmotivated to handle this critical area of their lives? What was holding them back from taking the relatively simple measures that would ensure a better financial future for themselves and their families?

Using my background in sociology and my years of study in personal development, I began to search for the reasons. Over the past few years I have uncovered a whole range of cultural beliefs—what I call "barriers"—that keep many Latinos from taking the small steps necessary to achieve long-term financial security and success. *The Latino Journey to Financial Greatness* is written to help change those beliefs and offer a new way for Latinos to increase the quality of their life while attaining financial greatness.

In the course of over 17 years in the financial planning industry, I have had many clients who have very few resources and are still very happy. I also have many wealthy clients who are searching for happiness and telling me that something is missing in their lives. Finally, most of my clients have a hard time making ends meet. They constantly struggle with the day-to-day stuff and are too busy to focus on what's really important. They work *in* their life but have no time to work *on* their life. I once heard a very profound quote in church: "If the devil doesn't make you bad, he makes you busy." It seems that we are all just too busy, and this busyness creates unfocused and unbalanced lives. It puts obstacles in our path and keeps us from getting to our ideal destination. We end up on the road to nowhere—to an unfulfilled life.

I believe everyone, especially Latinos, deserves something better. We have enormous strength of character and a rich cultural and social heritage that we can draw upon to make our dreams come true. We just need three simple things. First, we need to get out of our own way, to eliminate the few cultural beliefs and barriers that prevent us from recognizing our own financial strengths. Second, we need to understand the basics of making the most of our financial resources. And third, we need a little courage, a willingness to step forward and claim our position as a cultural and financial force in society. I believe you wouldn't be reading this book if you weren't ready for financial greatness. I will be honored if you let me be your guide.

Part One

The Road to Financial Greatness—and the Potholes Along the Way

When I left the prominent accounting and consulting firm I was working with in Newport Beach to open my own financial planning firm in the barrio of East Los Angeles, my colleagues thought I was crazy. "Your clients here are multimillionaires!" they said. "How many people in the barrio have money to invest in anything other than a roof over their heads and food on the table? Why do you think there's a need for financial planners in East L.A.?"

I knew because I grew up here. Like so many other Latinos, my father worked for years to save enough money to open his own business. Then, in addition to feeding and sheltering his family, he worked even harder to make sure that business was successful. Today I help people just like my father reach their financial dreams faster and more easily. I show them how to use banks, loans, insurance, investments, retirement accounts, and so on, and to create short- and long-range financial plans. I help Latinos achieve the financial greatness they dream of for themselves and their families.

What is financial greatness? Financial greatness goes beyond wealth. Financial greatness is having the courage to live the life of your dreams. Financial greatness is living a significant and purposeful life. Financial greatness is absolutely knowing that your life matters. Financial greatness is an abundance of love, confidence, and money. Financial greatness is living free of worry and struggle. In truth, financial greatness is at its core a mindset, one that can only be obtained with a clear vision of who you want to become, not just what things you want to have. In the September 2001 issue of *O* magazine, Oprah Winfrey said, "Everyone has the power for greatness—not for fame but for greatness, because greatness is determined by service."

Getting my clients to recognize their capacity for financial greatness, however, hasn't been easy. Even though Latinos as a group are hard-working and dedicated to supporting themselves and their families, even though they want to make the most of the opportunities offered to them, many people have never even considered how to make the best use of all the money they are earning. "I only bring home $750 a week," they tell me. "I'm supporting a family. I also send money to my relatives in Mexico (or Puerto Rico, or Central America, or elsewhere). Why would I need a financial plan?"

When I hear that, I know these people have bought into the belief of the "poor Latino." Sure, there are many poor Latinos living in the barrios of East L.A., Houston, Dallas, San Antonio, San

Francisco, Denver, Chicago, Miami, New York, and other U.S. cities. But in the same way that most people have no clue how much money they will earn and spend over the course of a lifetime (hint: it's something like $1.5 million), Latinos as a group have no clue how enormous our financial clout is and how much money we actually control.

Let me give you some facts that might help you realize how rich and powerful Latinos are.

▶ **We are the fastest-growing minority group in the United States, on track to become the biggest minority group in this country in less than 10 years.**
If the Latinos in the United States formed their own country, it would be the fifth largest Latin American country in the world.

▶ **We are a young population.**
The U.S. Census Bureau says the median age of Latinos is 26. This means more of our earning, spending, and childbearing years are ahead of us.

▶ **We have a lot of economic clout.**
Hispanic buying power reached $477 billion in the year 2000 and will only continue to grow.

▶ **We are an increasing presence in business.**
From 1987 to 1995, the number of Latino-owned businesses grew from 250,000 to 720,000—an increase of 288 percent.

▶ **We are an increasing presence in politics.**

Hispanics are recognized as one of the fastest-growing and most important voting blocs and are being courted aggressively by both Democrats and Republicans.

▶ **We are moving rapidly into the middle and upper classes.**

The fastest-growing segment of the Latino market is households with annual incomes of $50,000 or more.

As a group, Latinos are far from poor. However, I believe our greatest wealth isn't just in our pocketbooks, or in the paychecks we bring in each week or month. It's in our attitudes, in the way we look at work and family and community. In the next several chapters of this book I'm going to talk a lot about the beliefs and attitudes that get in the way of achieving financial greatness. But first I want to explode completely the myth of the "poor" Latino by reminding you of all the reasons we should be grateful for all that we have.

▶ **We are rich in family.**

Our family relationships are one of the strongest elements in our lives. In a society where it's very common for families to separate and lose touch, Latinos place enormous importance on taking care of people who are related to them. You will rarely see Latinos parked in a nursing home somewhere because their children are "too busy" to take care of them anymore. We care for our parents, our children, our brothers, sisters, aunts, uncles, and cousins. If a Latino or Latina immigrates to the United States, often they will spend their first few months or even years with a relative who gives them food and shelter and shows them how to get around.

► We are rich in community.

Our language, heritage, and culture bind us together and add dimension to our lives. Institutions like the church, sports, even Spanish-language television help keep us together and support us in taking pride in our identity as Hispanic Americans.

► We are rich in language.

Not only are there books, TV shows, entire industries conducted in Spanish in this country, but our fluency in both English and Spanish actually makes us *more* desirable in today's global marketplace. As everything becomes more and more globalized, the ability to both speak more than one language and move comfortably in different societies gives us a huge advantage.

► We are rich in our culture.

Pop music, TV, film, dance—the Latino influence is everywhere. And since we are a young population, this influence will only grow.

► We are rich in our attitudes about work.

Most Latino immigrants come to this country because we want to do better financially for ourselves and our families. We *want* to work, we *want* to earn a better living than we could in Mexico, or in Central or South America. And we're willing to take whatever work we can find just to make ends meet. Here in

Los Angeles you will rarely see a Latino begging for money. Instead, you'll see him or her selling bags of oranges, or flowers, or anything else they can. You'll see men standing around truck and equipment rental stores, asking not for a handout but for an honest day's work. We take whatever jobs we can, and we work hard to support ourselves and our families.

Family, community, language, culture, attitudes about work—in all those areas, Latinos have many advantages that drive us to make the most of whatever opportunities we have to build financial greatness. But in the same way that we can be sabotaged by the myths about Latinos that we encounter, all too often we sabotage *ourselves*—with our beliefs about money, our abilities, and what's possible and impossible for us. The next several chapters are designed to show you where these destructive beliefs came from and how the truth will set you free to build your own financial greatness more easily and quickly than you ever thought possible.

The Road to Financial Greatness

The road to financial greatness has five stages. Like any other road, some people may start at the very beginning, while others join the road closer to the goal. Here's what happens at each stage of the journey.

Survival Stage At this stage most people have a hard time coping with life. They are just figuring out where they are going to eat or sleep that day. People in this stage have trouble making plans more than a day or a week into the future.

Struggle Stage Here people have gotten past survival stage. They have food on the table and a roof over their heads, but a job loss or a large financial crisis will immediately take them into the survival stage again.

Stability Stage At this stage people have figured out how to maintain a roof over their heads, they have plenty of food on the table, and they even have enough money to occasionally take a vacation and begin to save for the future.

Success Stage This stage represents abundance. People have enough to be more than comfortable. They own their own home and a nice automobile; they have retirement savings and money set aside for their children's education; they can afford all the little extras they ever wanted. Unfortunately, at this point many people wake up and realize that the most important things in life aren't possessions. They ask, "Is this all there is?" They realize that something is missing; and when they find it, they reach the true goal of the journey . . .

Financial Greatness This occurs when people know their lives have purpose. Life works effortlessly. Relationships work. People who achieve financial greatness have an abundance of money, time, vitality, and love.

If we're lucky, most of us never have to go through the survival stage, where we don't even have a roof over our head. Many of us do go through the struggle stage when we're first starting out, and then hopefully we keep moving on to stability, success, and ultimately financial greatness. Most people believe that to get to financial greatness we have to pass through each stage of the road. But while each stage may have something important to teach us, I am suggesting that we can bypass some of the steps of the journey to financial greatness simply by knowing *what* to do and *when* to do it. I believe we can learn lessons from the struggles of others, and use what we learn to shorten our journey to financial greatness. But we have to be willing to listen and learn and then put what we learn into practice.

After over 17 years as a financial planner, I have found that it doesn't take a lot to be financially great. If you were to start putting aside $2 a day when you were 20 years old and kept doing so throughout your working life, and if that money were to earn 12 percent interest a year, by the time you were 65 you'd have over $1 million to retire on. But when it comes to financial greatness, the question is never, "How much money do you have saved?" but "Are you living a life of purpose, one where abundance flows naturally? Do you know who you are, what you have money for, and why?" The clients I see who are truly on the path to financial greatness are happy not because they have money but because they know why they earned the money to begin with. Their greatness comes not from finances but from themselves. I have written this book to show Latinos how truly great we are, and how financial abundance can be simply another manifestation of what we already have within. And ultimately, that greatness is a treasure no one can ever steal or spend or lose.

The Blindness of Bad Beliefs

Where does financial greatness start? From within—from the heart and mind rather than the pocketbook. But some of us—indeed, many people, not just Latinos—are blind to our own inner treasures. We can't see our resources—our strength, focus, creativity, discipline, and diligence—because we have been trained from the cradle to believe that's not who we are. And so we struggle along under an enormous burden of limiting beliefs and devastating doubts, not seeing the very things that could help us along our way.

Let me tell you a story that illustrates what I mean. Once there was a poor farmer who earned his living on a little plot of land near a remote village. His wife had passed away many years earlier, leaving him with a son. The boy was the apple of his father's eye; there was nothing the farmer would not do for his child.

One day the farmer had to go into the city to sell some of the produce from his farm. While he was gone, the village was attacked by bandits. When the farmer returned, he found the whole village in turmoil. He ran to his farm and was horrified to see his house had been burned to the ground. He sifted through the rubble and found the charred remains of the body of a child.

The farmer's grief knew no bounds. It was days before the other villagers could persuade him to bury the few pitiful bones he had found. Even when the child's remains had been laid to rest, the farmer kept one small bone for himself. He put the bone into a pouch and wore it around his neck at all times. Night after night, he would weep over the bone he believed to be a relic of his beloved son.

But the son had *not* died in the fire—the bones were those of another child. The marauders had kidnapped the farmer's young son and put him to work as their slave. Shortly afterward, the marauders had gone to the far north of the country, taking the boy with them. For years the boy worked in the camp and bided his time. Finally, he escaped. However, as he was a long way from home and had nothing but the clothes on his back, he went into the closest city to find work and earn enough money to return home. He approached a man who bought and sold cattle and asked him for a job. The man, who liked the boy's independent air, agreed to take him on. As the boy grew to young manhood, he became the cattle merchant's right hand.

After several years, the young man had made enough money to return home. So he told the cattle merchant his history of being kidnapped and separated from his father many years ago. "I am grateful to you for everything you have done for me, but now I wish to return home," he said. The cattle merchant was sad but agreed to the young man's request, and sent him on his way with many gifts and good wishes.

It took the young man many days to travel from the cattle merchant's city to his father's village. It was very late at night when he arrived at the house that his father had built to replace the one the marauders had burned those many years ago. The young man was happy and excited as he knocked on the front door.

"Who is it?" the father said from inside.

"Papa, open the door, it's your son!" the young man answered.

There was silence for a moment, then the father replied, with great sadness, "That's not possible."

The young man was surprised. He knocked again, saying, "Papa, it's true—I've returned home. I was taken by the men who burned our village. They made me their slave and took me to the far north. Finally, I escaped, but I had no way to come back. Since then I have been working for a merchant in the north to earn my way. I have gifts and money, enough to support us both. Papa, please open the door!"

"You are lying!" the father shouted angrily from inside the house. "I buried the bones of my son many years ago. I keep one bone with me to remember him by. It hangs in a pouch around my neck. You cannot be my son—either I'm having a dream or you're an evil spirit, here to take my soul. Devil, be gone! You are not my son."

No matter how much the young man pleaded, how many times he pounded, or how many tears he shed, the father was adamant. He would not open the door, not even a crack, or look outside for a moment. Finally, the young man left in despair. He never returned to the village again. Because the father would not believe his son had returned, he never knew the joy of holding his real son in his arms. A year later, the old man died, mourning the death of someone who was still alive.

What does this story have to do with creating financial greatness for yourself and your family? Everything. When I came back to the barrio of East L.A. and started offering financial planning services to the Latino community, I noticed there was a lack of information and knowledge about finances. So I taught seminars to help my clients understand the fundamentals of handling their money. But I quickly discovered that the most serious barrier I faced was not a lack of knowledge about finances, but the *negative beliefs most Latinos have about money.*

Latinos are a very smart, hard-working, responsible people. We take great care of ourselves and our families. We look out for each other, our children, our parents, and our relatives. But along with these good aspects of our culture, there are also some negative elements. Primarily, these are beliefs—about ourselves, about money, about abundance—that get in our way when it comes to making the most of our financial resources. Our beliefs dictate not only what we are willing to do but also what we are willing to accept as reality. Our beliefs can keep us from taking advantage of opportunities that are right in front of us. Just like the farmer with his son, even when opportunity comes pounding at our door we close our ears and say, "Evil spirit, go away!"

The first part of this book shows you the cultural beliefs that many Latinos have about money, and how to eliminate the negative ones so you can take advantage of opportunity when it comes along. That's the most important step in learning how to handle your money successfully—but it's only the first step. You also need to *discover your own personal reasons for creating wealth*. After all, your reasons will be different from your brother's or your neighbor's or your sister-in-law's! And when you know why you want to be wealthy, you will be driven to create that kind of abundance. Finally, you need to *create a plan* that will give you your own version of financial greatness, of wealth, happiness, and abundance for yourself and your family. The second part will give you a 10-step process that you can use to discover your reasons for creating wealth, set clear financial goals, and then devise a plan that will make your goals a reality. If you follow these 10 steps, I believe you can achieve all the financial greatness you could ever want.

Let me tell you a different ending to the story of the farmer and his son. This time when the son returns, the father decides to overcome his belief in his son's death and flings open the door.

With one look he recognizes the young man as his missing child, and they fall into each other's arms. The young man enters the house and shows his father the gifts and money he has brought with him. "I will never leave you again, Papa!" he declares as his father weeps, this time for joy.

The young man invests his money wisely and uses the proceeds to buy more farmland. He and his father work side by side, improving the farm, buying more livestock. In a very few years the small, poor farm has been transformed into one of the largest and most prosperous in the area. The son falls in love and marries a local girl, and together they have many beautiful, healthy children.

Eventually the father retires, leaving his son to run the farm while he plays with his grandchildren. Many years later, the old man dies, with his son, daughter-in-law, grandchildren, and even great-grandchildren at his side. At his funeral the people in the village say, "This man was so fortunate. He truly had greatness in his life."

The farmer's choice is one we all face repeatedly in our journey to financial greatness. Do we close the door to our minds and hearts and cling to our own ideas of what should be, or do we open the door to the truth—and thereby discover our own financial greatness?

10 Potholes on the Road to Financial Greatness

If you think of financial greatness as the destination of the road, then I have uncovered 10 "potholes"—beliefs many Latinos share that damage our relationships to finances. These beliefs are based on hundreds of years of cultural conditioning from our homelands, churches, and families. Like most beliefs, they are so much a part of our culture that we don't even see them anymore, but that gives them much greater power to affect us for good and for ill.

Let me give you an example of the power of a cultural belief. A few years ago I spent my very first Christmas at my in-laws'. It was awesome; I'd never seen so much food in one place before. As I looked at the table filled with every kind of delicious food imaginable, I asked my wife what her favorite dish was. "The ham," Angie told me. "My mother's baked ham is the best I've ever tasted. It's even won awards in cooking contests." I didn't believe her—until after I tasted it. Yep, Angie's mom's ham was the best I'd ever tasted, too!

I asked Angie what the secret was. "Well, Mom always cuts the ends of the ham off before baking it," she said. I assumed that the ham was so delicious because the cut ends allowed the juices to flow in and around the ham. But I decided to ask Angie's mom, Maria, why cutting off the ends of the ham made such a big difference. "I'm not sure what cutting the ends off does," Maria replied. "My mother taught me to do it that way, and it always tastes so wonderful I'm not going to mess with the recipe."

That's not good enough, I thought. I really want to know why this ham is so delicious. Luckily, Christmas is a major event in Angie's household, and her whole family was there. So I asked Angie's grandmother, Petra, the secret of the delicious ham. "I grew up in Guadalajara, Mexico," Petra told me. "My family was very poor and we only had one baking pan. Once a year we would get a ham for Christmas, but the baking pan was so small I had to cut off the ends of the ham to make it fit."

"Does cutting off the ends make the ham taste so good?" I asked, amazed.

"Of course not," she answered. "Who told you that?"

"Well, both your daughter and granddaughter are under the impression that it does," I said.

Petra laughed. "Cutting the ends off a ham is just a habit that I never thought to change," she said. "The real reason my ham is so delicious is the combination of Mexican spices I bake it with."

"Do you think we should tell Angie and Maria?" I asked.

Petra looked at me, a twinkle in her eye. "We'd better—think of all the good ham our family has wasted over the years!"

We need to be careful about what we believe to be true. Beliefs that are tied to our heritage, our family and our culture, are often very strong, but they are often based on the wrong information. And when we hold on to the wrong beliefs, we can make wrong assumptions about what makes someone or something truly great. Then we keep doing things the same way we've always done them, instead of exploring other ways to get better results.

The real problem, of course, arises when our wrong beliefs aren't about things like baking hams but about ourselves, our abilities, and what it will take for us to accomplish what we want for ourselves financially. I see the power of such barriers in my office every single day with clients who don't believe they can be financially secure. I see them in my seminars, where I talk about these barriers and see heads nodding throughout the room in agreement. Most of all, I see these barriers in action in homes, on the streets, and in the banks and car lots and real estate offices—wherever Latinos do business. I have seen how these cultural beliefs keep us from taking advantage of some of the most basic and effective tools for building financial greatness for ourselves and our families.

Exposing and eliminating these beliefs were two reasons why I started offering financial education seminars. It's also one of the reasons I wrote a regular financial column called "Entre Numeros" (Between the numbers) in *La Opinion,* Los Angeles's largest Spanish-language newspaper, for 5 years. And it's why the first half of this book isn't about how to set up a retirement account or save for your children's education or get a better job or pick a financial adviser. Instead, you're going to learn about some cultural beliefs that are the Latino version of cutting the ends off the ham—false ideas that are getting in our way as we journey to financial greatness.

What you read in this section may surprise you. It may even anger you. If an Anglo were saying this to a Latino, you'd probably say, "Oh, he's just a racist." You may feel that I am even putting my own people down and buying into the cultural stereotypes of Latinos. But even though I'm Latino, born and raised in East L.A., I've also lived and worked in the Anglo community. I've seen how Anglos and Latinos approach handling their money, and I've made careful note of the differences. To understand where these differences came from, I've done research into the history and culture of Latinos. Based on what I learned, I came to recognize how our history has created these 10 barriers. Since then, I've studied sociology, psychology, and personal development to try and figure out why these barriers affect us so deeply, and, most important, how to eliminate the negative effects of these barriers forever.

My purpose here is not just to show you how your relationship to money may be shaped by these 10 barriers; it's to help you educate your children and grandchildren so they can take advantage of all the enormous financial opportunities available to them. Ultimately, my goal is to empower the Latino community. As long as we are held by these cultural beliefs, there will be people—Latinos, Anglos, members of every possible race or ethnic background—who will be happy to take advantage of us. But with a little knowledge and awareness of how we've been trained to think, and with a determination to break out of those old patterns, we can start to take charge of our own financial futures. And with clear vision, we can truly create financial greatness for ourselves, our children, and our community as a whole.

So, here are the 10 barriers. As you read about each one, don't just think about whether you have these beliefs yourself. Ask, "How have I seen these beliefs in my parents? My neighbors? My children? How have I and the people I know been affected by this barrier?" Then take a moment to decide if you want to keep believing it. If you want to do so, fine. I'm certainly not here to tell you that there's only one way to believe. But please, first consider what this barrier may cost you if you continue to hold on to it, and what a new belief might give you should you choose to try it on.

After all, the freedom to choose what we believe is one of the reasons millions of people come to the United States. But here's the secret: *We can also choose to change our beliefs if they don't support us.* The choices you make about these barriers may shape your financial future for good or ill. So please choose well, because you need to know that your choices will have long-term consequences.

Let's begin the journey!

Barrier #1

The Patron-Peon *System:* Depending on Others to Take Care of You

Until very recently, many Latin American countries had primarily agricultural societies, where most people worked the land. But the land was actually owned by someone else—the *patron*. The *patron* was the most powerful figure in the area. He had the land, the money, the connections with officials. However, he needed a lot of people just to maintain his estates, so he would use all his power and influence to make sure that the only choice for the peasants nearby was to work for him. He would buy up land, drive other farmers out, and use all sorts of other tactics until most people decided, "It's better for me to work for the *patron* and have a little than to go out on my own and possibly have more. I'm afraid that if I go out on my own I'll never be able to make it." So even though the *patron-peon* system provided some kind of minimal economic benefit for employees, it never gave them the chance to break out of dependence and take off on their own.

However, there was an upside to the *patron-peon* system: The *patron* had a responsibility to take care of his workers, providing for their needs and looking out for them when they were in trouble. Since the *peons* knew they couldn't trust the government or any other big institution, they came to rely on the *patron* for everything. They depended upon the person with more wealth and power to help them out in times of trouble.

The cultural heritage of dependence built into the *patron-peon* system affects many Latinos to this day. Too often we are looking for someone else to take care of our needs rather than taking care of them ourselves. We don't take charge of our own finances, for example, because we figure the company, Social Security, our family, or some other mysterious "they" will look out for us. I believe the heritage of the *patron-peon* system is also one of the reasons some Latinos end up in the welfare system. A lot of families in low-income areas of Latino communities may view government assistance as the *patron* who is supposed to take care of them. That's the heritage of a culture of dependency.

Here's the other way the *patron-peon* system can affect Latinos: It can stifle our entrepreneurial desires and dreams. If the American dream is to own your own business, the dream for many parents in Latino communities is for their kids to go and work for a big company. Parents believe that, like the *patron,* the big company will take care of their kids. It will provide them with a steady income, perhaps promotions, certainly a pension. If their kids want to change jobs or go out and start a business of their own, the parents advise them against it. "It's too much of a risk," the older generation says. "Stay where it's safe."

Latino kids learn early and well the lesson that someone will take care of them. So well, in fact, that many Latinos stay with their parents far into their twenties. As the Latino comedian George Lopez says in one of his routines: "You know why there aren't any homeless Latinos? Because Latinos never leave home." Unfortunately, this tendency never to leave home isn't just a reflection of the closeness of Latino families; it's actually an indication of the dependence of Latino kids. They go to work right out of high school or after a little college, but they have to live at home because they don't earn a lot. Even when they get married and have kids, they stay with their parents because they can't afford to move out. "We'll just stay until we save enough for a down payment on a house," the kids say—but they never do. Instead, they party their extra money away because their basic needs are taken care of. They don't have a long-term perspective or any need to be accountable. Why should they? Their parents are taking care of them, and eventually, they think, their own kids will do the same.

Patron-peon thinking also affects more responsible Latinos. Many aging Latino parents rely on their children to take care of them. You rarely see Latinos in old-age homes or extended-care facilities because the culture dictates that the family—*la familia*—takes care of its own no matter what. Unfortunately, the people who are supposed to be taking care of aging parents are also usually raising their own children at the same time. They become a "sandwich generation," squeezed between the financial and time crunches of aging parents and growing children. "I will never be a burden to my kids," these people usually vow, only to fall back into the same cultural pattern when they reach old age themselves.

In today's economy, obviously the *patron-peon* way of doing things is a hundred years out of date. There is no official *patron* in the United States to take care of any of us—Latino, Anglo, or any other cultural group. Social Security won't do it; not only was Social Security never designed to be anyone's main source of retirement income, but many sources tell us that there won't be enough money to cover the needs of retirees by the year 2038. And those big-company pensions and retirement benefits . . . well, as people who worked for Kodak, Polaroid, Enron, TWA, and WorldCom know, the promises of retirement income and the actual payout when the time comes can be very different. In fact, most U.S. workers won't spend enough time at one company even to be *eligible* for a pension. Most of us will have three or four different careers and 10 different jobs over the course of a working lifetime. Add to that the fact that every generation is living longer: According to projections, a child born today is likely to live to age 102. Even those of us who were born in the twentieth century will live longer due to new drugs, better treatments for illness, and so on. If we retire at age 55 (as most of us would like to), we can anticipate 25, 30, even 40 years during which we will need to support ourselves without working. And I don't know about you, but I don't want to be a burden on my kids (or society) for 25 or more years.

What all this means is, *we have to take financial responsibility for ourselves and our future, starting now.* We have to start saving for retirement as soon as possible. We have to make our own plans and not rely on our parents, children, employer, or the government to take care of us. I advise my clients to take advantage of the retirement plans offered by most employers. Not "pension plans"—as I said earlier, you can't rely on a company to pay you a pension—but 401(k) and other retirement plans where you put a certain amount each year into a special account. You don't have to pay taxes on that money until you withdraw it (which hopefully won't be until you retire), and many employers have programs where they will match your contribution (putting in as much money as you do).

By the way, some of my clients don't participate in the 401(k) plans offered at their jobs because they're afraid that the company will have some "claim" on that money, or that if the company goes out of business the 401(k) money will vanish, too. But nothing could be farther from the truth. Any money you put into a 401(k) is yours. The only way it could vanish is if you put it into bad investments. And I hope that by the end of this book you'll be able to choose your investments a little more wisely.

To take care of ourselves financially, however, we have to be willing to take some risks. One of the best ways to become wealthy and make the most of the opportunities available in the United States is to start your own business; but there are a lot of risks in becoming an entrepreneur, and it's difficult for many people (not just Latinos) to take that leap. To make the most of our opportunities, to get the greatest financial benefit from the money we earn, we have got to get rid of the idea that anyone but us will take care of us. We have to run the show ourselves, and actively seek the help we need to do so in the best way we can. We have to become the *patron* of our own finances, careers, and futures.

Barrier #2

Mattresses and Mayonnaise Jars: Storing Rather Than Investing Money

Frequently clients come into my office with wads of cash in their hands. "I need to invest this," they say. "My parent (or grandparent) died recently, and we found all this money hidden underneath the mattress." One man found $25,000 that had been hidden away in several coffee cans by his grandmother—who had died four years earlier!

Where do you keep your money? If you're like many Latinos, you start by putting all your spare change in mayonnaise jars. Then you graduate to a big 5-gallon water bottle. (My parents have two 5-gallon water bottles, one filled with pennies, and one with quarters, dimes, and nickels. The bottles are so heavy they can't lift them to take them to the bank!) Eventually you convert your change into bills and put them under the mattress or in the bottom of a cookie jar or container of flour. And if you finally decide to invest it, the most you'll do is take your cash to the local bank and put it into a low-paying savings account.

Why? With all the different kinds of investments available through banks and brokers and financial advisers, why do so few Latinos take advantage of commonplace financial instruments like stocks, bonds, mutual funds, and so on? This was an important question to me, a financial adviser, so I started asking people in my community what exactly was going on, people like my father, a businessman who has lived in East L.A. for 47 years. And I concluded that the primary reason many Latinos keep their money in mayonnaise jars and underneath their mattresses is a *lack of information and education about finances.*

Latinos understand money; we're very good at managing it, saving it, budgeting it, even sending it back to support relatives in our native countries. But like many people, we are afraid to put our hard-earned money into things we don't understand. So we go to the local bank and open up a checking or savings account (which pays almost no interest) because we know that anytime we want we can walk into the bank and get our money. That's easy to understand and manage.

With stocks or bonds or many other investments, however, we can't see our money being invested anywhere unless we've bought shares or bonds in a local business. We're uncomfortable with financial instruments like bonds or stocks because they are just "pieces of paper" or lines on an account statement. Unless we really understand the benefits of investing, why in the world would we want to take money we can see and put it someplace we can't?

But there is one kind of investment that most Latinos will make. Since we want to put our money into something tangible, we buy real estate—something we can see, walk on, and drive our families by as we point to it with pride. I also think this tendency to buy real estate comes from the primarily agricultural background of the countries that many Latino immigrants come from. Land has always represented wealth, so we believe that owning real estate is the best way to become wealthy.

Of course, real estate has a place in many financial plans. I'm a firm believer in home ownership, or in owning the property and buildings where your small business is located (if that makes good business sense). But real estate should not be the only investment you make. There are a lot of other kinds of investments that can produce much greater returns in a much shorter period of time.

Here's the truth about mattresses and mayonnaise jars: *The smartest place to put your money isn't necessarily where you can see it, but where you know what it's doing.* With just a little education and effort, it's possible for your hard-earned money to work a lot harder for you *and* be a lot safer than it would be in a jar or invested only in one place. The question isn't, "Where will my money be safe?" but "What do I need to know in order to have my money give me the greatest return with the amount of risk I'm comfortable with?"

Three Categories of Investments

Understanding money doesn't have to be difficult. There are a few simple concepts we need to learn so we can figure out where to put our money once we get beyond the "spare change" stage. Basically, there are only three types of core investments: cash, fixed, and equity.

► Cash

Everyone should have a certain amount of cash accessible for emergencies and general expenses, but that doesn't mean you have to stash it under the mattress. There are several kinds of investments where you can get your money immediately, yet you still earn interest and dividends on what you've invested. Cash investments can be actual cash, savings accounts, money market accounts, short-term (less than a year) certificates of deposit or CDs, money market funds, and U.S. treasuries. All of these investments have high liquidity (meaning you can turn them into cash at a moment's notice) and carry very little risk that you will lose money on the investment.

► Fixed Investments

With these, you lend your money to an organization or an individual, and they return it after a specified time period. In the meantime you receive interest or dividends at a higher rate than you would receive with cash instruments because you lock in your money for a longer time. Fixed investments include long-term bonds (government, municipal, and corporate), bond mutual funds, second-trust deeds, and any other long-term loan.

With fixed investments, you get a greater rate of return, but you lose liquidity—you can't get your money out of them as quickly as you can with cash investments. And the principal fluctuates with interest rate changes. With bonds or any type of fixed investments, when interest rates go up, the principal (the face value of the bond, deed, loan, etc.) goes down, and vice versa. Therefore, if you sell the bond, you may have to sell it for less than you would receive if you held it until it matured. You may also be assessed a penalty for cashing in early. Fixed investments are great for guaranteed income but not for long-term investing.

► **Equity investments**

When you make an equity investment, instead of lending, you are *owning.* You buy something—stock, or a piece of real estate, or gold—for a certain price because you believe that something will become more valuable over time. However, the price of that investment goes up or down depending on the market. As the owner of that investment, you are taking all the risk.

The way most people can understand equity investments is to think of them as a house. When you buy a house, the amount you pay for it will depend on the current market, right? And if you want to sell that house in five years, can you predict today how much that house will be worth then? Of course not. But here's the great thing about equity investments: greater risk can mean greater reward. Say the neighborhood your house is in has become very popular in the five years since you bought it. Houses exactly like yours on the same street are now selling for twice what you paid 5 years ago. You've doubled your money because the market has changed in your favor. That's what can happen with equity investments.

Some examples of equity investments are stocks, equity mutual funds, real estate, precious metals, and collectibles. These types of investments don't earn a consistent rate of return, and the value of your principal (the money you put into the investment) can fluctuate up or down. Using the

house example, suppose your neighborhood got a lot worse—
is it possible that your house would then be worth *less* than you
paid for it? Unfortunately, yes. That's what I mean when I say
the value of your principal can go up or down.

You can sell equity investments pretty much anytime you
want, but it will be at whatever price the market wishes to pay.
You may end up taking a loss simply because it's a bad time to
sell that particular stock or mutual fund or piece of property.
Because equity investments provide the greatest rate of return
on your money, you can do very well with them as part of your
long-term portfolio. However, the potential for losing your
money is also higher.

Which of the three types of investments is best? As much as
investment companies or financial salespeople would like you to
think so, there is no such thing as a perfect investment. All investments have some level of risk; all investments have advantages
and disadvantages. But what you decide to put your money into
should be based on the following four questions. (In Part 2, we'll
also go through an entire 10-step process that will help you create
a financial plan for yourself.)

First, *what are your investment goals?* One of your goals should
be to save for retirement, but putting all your retirement money
under the mattress would be pretty silly. Even if you were to put
that money in a savings account, you'd at least be earning a little
interest on it. For long-term retirement planning, you want to
put your money where it can grow as much as possible until you
need it. Suppose, however, your goal is to have an emergency
fund so you could still pay the family bills for a few months if you
got hurt on the job. You wouldn't want to put that money into

real estate, for example, because you might not be able to get the cash quickly enough. The investments you choose need to fit what you want the money for.

Second, *how soon (or how quickly) will you need the money?* If you just started working and want to save for retirement, putting money into equities may be a great way to invest your retirement fund. But suppose you're saving for your daughter's wedding. She just turned 21 and has a serious boyfriend, so you're probably going to need the money in two or three years. A fixed investment like a bond that won't let you get your money for another five years wouldn't work. Neither would putting your money into stocks or a piece of real estate and hoping that the market will be high when you need to sell. In this case, the best investment might be in the highest-paying money market account, or a bank CD that pays a specific interest and matures (that is, you can cash it out without penalty) in a year or two. When choosing investments, you should always be very clear about when you will need the money you're investing.

Third, *how comfortable are you with these investments?* How much do you know about the investment you want to make? So many clients come to me and say, "I'm not invested in any stocks," and yet in their 401(k) retirement plan they have stock mutual funds. When I tell them, "Some of your mutual funds are made up of different stocks," they look at me in complete surprise. I also see this lack of understanding with clients who come to me after consulting with other financial salespeople. "My brother-in-law's guy told me to put my money into gold futures," they'll say. "Now he says I've lost 80 percent of my investment. How can that happen?"

I'm not saying you have to be an expert in bonds or stocks to put your money into savings bonds or IBM stock, but you should know *something* about whatever it is you're investing in. I hope this book will provide you with the basics, but if you don't understand an investment, either take the time to learn enough about it so you're comfortable with putting your money there or choose something else. There are lots of great investments that anyone can understand, but *you* have to take the responsibility for asking questions and getting the information you need.

When you're seeking to understand investments, beware of taking the advice of so-called investment "experts" who offer free advice on the Internet, the talk shows, in books, on TV and radio. It's very easy to get taken in by what I call investment "noise." What experts tell you to do may not work in your particular situation. Also, most of the time all you're hearing is a "sound bite," a quick sentence or two that is easy for most of us to misinterpret. I know, because I speak on Spanish-language television here in L.A. all the time. The station gives me 2 minutes to explain what's going on in the market—but who can explain finances in 2 minutes? No one can. I try to encapsulate my own understanding in a very few words, but I say repeatedly that my comments are not designed to be financial advice. However, I worry that some people may still hear me and say, "Louis said drug company stocks are doing well, so I'm going to buy some," when that's not what I really meant.

I know of several people who bought into mutual funds run by very well known media financial "experts" and lost their shirts. Experts don't have all the answers. If they did, they'd be so rich they probably wouldn't still be offering advice. Don't listen to the investment noise. Yes, you can listen and learn basic principles from financial experts, as I hope you'll learn from me. But I wouldn't dare make specific recommendations for your investment dollars in this book. Find a financial professional (see Barrier #3) who will give you advice tailored to your specific goals, timeline, and knowledge. And make sure you understand their recommendations before you put a dime into anything.

Fourth, *how much risk are you willing to take?* Every investment carries some risk with it. Even if you put your money in the mattress, you could have a fire or a robbery and lose everything. If you put your money in a guaranteed bank account with a good interest rate, the bank could still go out of business. Or interest rates could change: When the Federal Reserve lowered interest rates 11 times in 2001, the amount of interest banks were offering on money market accounts dropped as low as 2.0 percent—almost the same as a regular savings account and not much better than putting the money in your mattress! The value of the investment could also change depending on market conditions. People used to think of utility stocks as a very safe investment, but then the market changed (especially here in California) and utility stocks lost a lot of their value.

No matter whether you put your money in cash, fixed investments, or equities, there will always be some risk. In truth, the greatest risk can come from playing it too safe, because you're guaranteed that your money is going to keep losing value simply because of inflation. (Inflation is the amount the cost of living goes up each year. It means that the money you save for the future won't buy as much when that future arrives. For example, $100 in 2002 buys a lot less than $100 bought in 1990.) Risk is something we have to understand, accept, and learn to manage. We can even learn to use risk to our advantage. For example, if you're 25 years old and investing for retirement, you can take a little more risk because you have a longer time to make up for any losses you might take. But the best way to lessen the "risk of risk" is to invest your money in different things—in other words, to diversify.

The Key to Financial Strength: Diversification

There's a saying in English: "Don't put all your eggs in one basket." Why not? Because if something happens to the basket, you'll lose all your eggs. Diversification prevents you from losing your "eggs"—the money you've worked so hard to earn. If you put your money into different kinds of investments (*not* different versions of the same thing), even if something goes wrong in one investment, the money you have in the other kinds should be okay.

Think of it this way. Suppose you invested all your money in a rental property and then the building burned down, or the tenants trashed it so it lost a lot of its value. If instead you had bought a less expensive property and invested the rest of your money in stocks, bonds, or mutual funds, you'd still have some of your money left. One investment can go down to nothing, but the others will probably still be earning you money.

A good financial adviser will usually encourage you to spread your money around by putting some of it into each of the three categories of investments: cash, fixed investments, and equities. That way, no matter what the markets and banks are doing, your money is probably going to be okay (remembering, still, that every investment has some amount of risk). When you speak to your adviser, make sure you understand the recommendations that are being made to you, and what category of investment this chunk of money is going into. I see a lot of people walk into my office and say proudly, "My 401(k) is diversified. I have money in 20 different mutual funds!" Yet when I look at the funds they've got, they're all made up of similar stocks. That's not diversification. Remember the categories:

- **Cash**: savings accounts, bank CDs, money market accounts, money market funds
- **Fixed investments**: government, municipal, and corporate bonds; bond mutual funds; second trust deeds
- **Equity investments**: stocks, stock mutual funds, gold, collectibles, real estate

When you're diversified, you've got money in each category. Instead of putting all your eggs in one basket, you've got some in the basket you're carrying, some stashed away where you can get at them at a moment's notice, and some put away making you lots of money for the future. If you start out with a good financial adviser who will help you get clear, then you'll know where your money is. You'll understand the investments you've made and how much you're making on them. You'll be fully prepared to travel the road to financial greatness.

Barrier #3

Mi Compadre: Consulting (Non) Experts

I n most Latino countries, whenever a child is born the parents select a godparent (or godparents) for that child. And since the godparent is responsible for taking care of the child if anything happens to its parents, often the parents ask the most financially secure or successful person they know to be the godfather—the *compadre*. The godfather is supposed to look out for that child, to be there for him or her whenever that child needs help.

But here's how this *compadre* relationship evolved over time. In the community there would be one or two well-known, financially successful people—the local merchant, or someone who runs a profitable business or a manufacturing plant. This person would become the *compadre* for all of his friends, associates, and relatives. And because he was successful, others would come to him for financial advice, even if it was about something in which the *compadre* had no expertise.

Let me give you an example. A young man I knew became very successful in sports. He was making a lot of money and wanted some advice about what to do with it. The young man's father had as his *compadre* a man who owned a successful used-car business. This man knew a lot about building and running his business, but he knew nothing about investing. Instead of going to a professional financial adviser, however, the young man went to the *compadre*. And unfortunately, he lost a lot of money as a result.

Culturally we Latinos rely on people we know, even if that person is not an expert in the area we need advice in. This absolutely affects where and how we invest our money. As a culture we are comfortable with investing in our homes, in property, in assets we can see and touch, so one of the most common professionals you'll find in the Latino community is a real estate agent. Because many of these agents are seen as successful and financially aware, people who are looking for a *compadre* to give them financial advice will go to the realtor. And of course, just as a surgeon will tell you that you need surgery and the insurance agent will tell you that you need insurance, the real estate agent will tell you that you need to buy property. Because we are consulting people who only know one thing, one area, we are never exposed to all the possibilities for investment that are available.

Here's the other thing that happens in Latino communities. In Mexico, as well as other Latin American countries, an attorney (someone who deals with the law) is called a *notario*. In the United States, a notary is someone who merely witnesses and confirms signatures on legal documents. But here's the confusion: many Latinos will go to a "notary" in their community, thinking this person is like an attorney. They will ask the notary for legal advice—and the notary oftentimes will give it to them! I've had several clients come to me with financial problems that are due to some legal difficulties. I'll say to them, "Who did you consult about this legal challenge?" and they'll reply, "I went to the *notario*, the notary."

There's a famous *dicho* (saying) in Spanish: "*Dime con quien andas y te dire quien eres*," which means, "Tell me who you hang out with and I'll tell you who you are." Nowhere is this truer than in your financial life. Tell me who you consult about your finances, and without knowing any more about you I can tell you what kind of financial life you have. And if we're dealing with an uncle who owns a used-car lot, or a bookkeeper, or a notary—instead of going to an accountant when we have an accounting problem, or an attorney for a legal problem, or a financial planner when we want to invest our money wisely—our results are going to reflect the level of (in)expertise of the person we consulted.

Unfortunately, in the barrio there have been very few professional financial advisers. The assumption in the financial community has been that Latinos don't have any financial needs because they lack resources. And what financial adviser wants to deal with clients who don't have any money to invest? But of course this is completely untrue. Latinos *do* have financial resources, and we have the same need for good, professional financial advice as anyone. Luckily, more and more financial professionals are realizing that there is an enormous market in our community, and they are starting to provide quality financial services for us.

Choosing a Good Financial Professional

However, as I said, we can only achieve a certain level of status or financial independence according to the people we hang out with and consult. And not all financial professionals are created equal. There are good accountants and bad accountants, good financial professionals and shoddy ones. You need to understand what to look for in your financial advisers. Remember, *you* are hiring *them*. Even if you think they know more than you about finances, it's still your money they will be dealing with. Therefore, you have to be comfortable with them, and also make sure they will do a good job for you. Luckily, you don't have to have a master's degree in business or finance to pick a great financial adviser. Here are some rules of the road to hiring any type of financial professional.

► **Hire financial advisers who are full-time professionals.**
In the barrio it is not uncommon to see advisers who are jacks-of-all-trades. You'll see a sign above a business saying the proprietor is a travel agent, real estate agent, mortgage broker, cellular phone representative, phone card salesperson, tax preparer, auto insurance salesperson, and notary. There is a saying, "*El que mucho abarca, poco aprieta*," which means that you can do very few things right if you try to do everything. When it comes to your money, you want someone who knows his or her stuff about just that—managing and investing money. Don't go with a jack-of-all-trades; hire financial advisers who are specialists in their own fields.

► **Look for competency, not price.**

Another saying tells us, *"Lo barato sale caro."* Loosely translated, this means you get what you pay for. A good adviser has probably spent a lot of time studying his or her field, getting degrees and certifications in different specializations. You want quality and competency when you entrust someone with your money, not the best "deal."

When hiring a financial adviser, look for years in the profession (experience), professional credentials attained, and a great reputation. Then look at what he or she charges. Most of the time, you'll find the higher fees are more than offset by better results—and greater peace of mind for you.

Now let's look at some don'ts when it comes to hiring a financial professional.

► **Don't hire someone who is just starting out in the financial advice profession or is doing it as a secondary, sideline business.**

As I said earlier, you want someone who is trained in finances and who focuses all his or her energy and time in that area. But you also don't want to be the guinea pig of someone who is just starting out. You are looking for someone with at least 5 years' experience. Why? Statistics show that 80 percent of people in the financial services industry leave the profession within 5 years. Your money is too important to allow someone to make his or her mistakes with it.

► **Don't hire someone who tells you he or she is an expert in the field and then tries to recruit you to become a salesperson for his company.**

In the last 10 years or so there have been a lot of financial multilevel marketing businesses, where one person sells you an insurance policy or mutual fund and then offers you incentives (like commissions and deep discounts) if you become a "salesperson," too. This is just a way for the salesperson to make extra money. They hope you will sell the policies to your family and friends, who will buy from you because of a sense of obligation. Instead of the person who sold to you having to do all the work of selling, you do it for them; and he or she then earns a commission from the sales you make.

The person who is more interested in recruiting salespeople isn't going to be looking out for your best financial interests when it comes to recommending financial services. If you want to get into the financial services business, great—go to school and become an accountant or financial adviser. If you want to be a salesperson, find a reputable company that offers good training and pays based on what you produce, not how many people you talk into becoming salespeople under you. But don't choose financial professionals who try to recruit you into their business. (By the way, I'm not saying all multilevel organizations are bad, but I don't think they belong in the financial services field.)

► **Don't hire a jack-of-all-trades.**

As I said earlier, it's impossible to be an expert in more than one field. (I occasionally have come across people who can be great at two, but this is extremely rare.) When someone is great at what they do, they don't need to earn income from multiple sources. If you choose a financial adviser who is trying to juggle five different careers, I assure you that you will never achieve financial greatness.

▶ Don't hire someone who doesn't tell you up front what he is going to charge you.

Any good financial adviser is going to need to be paid some-how. Even the ones who offer advice for "free" are making money, usually by earning a commission on what they sell you. Ask the financial professional how he will be paid. Is he going to charge you a commission, a flat fee, an hourly fee? You need to know what these services will cost you. Don't fall for the "It's not going to cost you anything, my company is going to pay me" trap. You always pay, one way or another, so it's better to know what the cost will be right at the start.

▶ Don't hire a family member.

This is a tough one for Latinos, because most of us have family as our highest value. But if you think family arguments over money are bad, try the arguments that break out when a family member gives you "professional" financial advice that doesn't work out! I have seen more family break-ups over this than any-thing else. Keep family and business separate! I refer family members to other planners. If they want, I will act as the second opinion. It's great going to Thanksgiving and not having to deal with 10 relatives whose portfolios are down 20 percent for the year. Family functions are much more pleasant when you keep this rule.

▶ Don't hire someone who promises you something that is too good to be true.

"You can double your money in a month." "This is a sure thing—there's absolutely no risk." "You could put all your money in this one investment and sleep soundly for the next

20 years." There is no such thing as a perfect, risk-free investment. Nothing is perfect. Nothing! Every investment has its good points and bad points. Make sure the professional explains them all to you to your satisfaction before you put a dime in. And remember to *always* get all promises in writing.

► **Don't hire a noncredentialed adviser.**
Credentials mean that someone has studied a particular kind of investing or financial service. Most people have heard the term CPA, which means certified public accountant. CPAs have spent several years in school and passed exams that entitle them to call themselves a CPA. There are credentials for financial planning (CFP™), for tax preparation (EA), for advising people in divorce financial matters and retirement issues, and so on. Most advisers will list their credentials on their business cards or in any written material about their business.

People who have credentials in the industry and specialty have made the effort to study for and pass rigorous exams. This doesn't assure you that they're any good, but it does promise you that they're better than someone who doesn't care about meeting at least minimum industry standards.

► **Don't choose someone based on a "cold call."**
If you've ever been interrupted right at dinnertime by someone who is trying to sell you insurance or offering you a hot stock tip, you've been subjected to a cold call. Don't hire anyone who calls you at your home in the evening without even knowing you. Trust me, competent advisers don't need to do this. Good advisers have plenty of work from the referrals they get from their current clients.

Some Suggestions for Choosing Specialists

Those are the basics to keep in mind when hiring any financial adviser. But depending on your needs, you may wish to consult a specialist. Here are a few of the specialties you may encounter, a general idea of the kind of services they offer, and tips for finding the best one for you.

Financial Planner

A financial planner will take a look at all of your finances and put together a plan that will help you meet your goals, including retirement, education for your children, and so on. Look for a financial planner who

- Is a certified financial planner (CFP^{TM}).
- Can provide you with different investment products from different investment companies.
- Prepares a financial plan specifically for you. Many financial plans are "boilerplate," meaning the planner simply plugs in a new name and then provides a standard set of recommendations. If your financial needs are very simple, that's fine. However, a good financial planner will take into account your specific situation and create a plan tailored to your needs. Have the financial planner show you a sample of two financial plans. Boilerplate plans will have the same wording except in just a very few areas. If the plans are very similar, trust me, this adviser is not likely to produce a plan designed just for you.

- Asks you questions about your short-term and long-term goals and takes into consideration what is important to you. If you are shown a product without a lot of prior conversation about your specific financial goals, I would consider working with someone else.
- Reviews *all* your investment, financial statements, and insurance policies, including employee benefits, before recommending any type of product to meet your needs.

Insurance Agent

An insurance agent specializes in advice about different kinds of insurance policies: life, disability, health, property, and casualty, and so on. When looking for an insurance agent, hire one who

- Can advise you about and sell competitive insurance products with different types of insurance companies. Rates and terms on policies will vary from company to company; you want an agent who will help you find the best policy for you, not the best policy his or her company offers.
- Reviews *all* your insurance needs. This includes health, life, disability, auto, homeowners, renters, long-term care, and umbrella.
- Doesn't see insurance as a solution to all your problems. Some agents will recommend that you put all your retirement money in an insurance policy that you can draw against after a specific age. As I said earlier, putting all your money in any one kind of investment is stupid. Any good insurance agent will be aware of the benefits of different investments.

- Focuses on your needs, not theirs. Some, not all, insurance agents will rationalize that they are doing what's best for you, while in truth they are lining their pockets by selling you insurance products that carry high commissions. If you feel this is the case, simply walk away. *No tengan vergüenza*—don't be embarrassed. You're taking care of your money in the most responsible way possible.

Tax Preparer

Depending on your financial situation, you may wish to have someone else prepare your personal or business tax returns. Since tax codes for the federal government change almost every year, and since the penalties for incorrect tax returns are very high, it's important that you find a good tax preparer who

- Is a full-time, licensed tax preparer, enrolled agent, or CPA. If you will need tax representation (that is, if you have been audited in the past or think you will be audited), stick to an enrolled agent or CPA who can go to the audit for you. If you have a situation involving legal issues, use a tax attorney.
- Has a reputation for preparing returns correctly, not for getting big tax refunds. Everybody hates overpaying taxes, but don't let greed overtake you by going with someone who tells you he knows "special" tax loopholes that no one else does. Always make sure the tax preparer signs the return, and then you review it for any suspicious deductions before submitting it. Bottom line,

you're responsible for the accuracy of everything you submit on the tax return. Claiming ignorance in an audit doesn't work.

Real Estate Agent

Because most of us will either buy or sell a home at least once in our lifetime, almost everyone deals with a real estate agent at one time or another. But since Latinos frequently choose to invest in property, you may find you need different agents for different types of properties. Look for a real estate agent who

- Specializes in the type of property you want to purchase.
- Specializes in the geographical area in which you want to purchase.
- Is ethical. I have seen too many Latinos get hurt by using real estate agents who falsify documents to have their clients qualify for a home. If someone tells you that they can help you get into a home because they have friends who can work magic (pull a *movida*), tell them politely that you are not interested.

Estate Planning Attorney

Eventually, most of us have to think about passing on our money and possessions—our estate—to our children, grandchildren, etc. An estate planning attorney has been trained to help you set up a plan (including a will and, if necessary, a trust) to be sure your money goes where you want it to. Hire an estate planning attorney who

- Is an estate planning specialist.
- Reviews your estate plan thoroughly and takes into consideration all your needs.
- Is objective and doesn't impose his or her beliefs on how you should transfer your assets.

"Dime con quien andas y te dire quien eres" also means that you are only as strong as your weakest link. It often surprises me how little thought we put into deciding who we want representing us. But remember, your financial advisers are a reflection of who you are and what you want. Choose trusted advisers with impeccable reputations in their profession and community. There are more and more highly competent, ethical professional advisers in the Latino community. But you have to do your homework to find them. Ask for referrals from people you trust and admire. Interview all financial professionals and ask questions. All truly good financial professionals want their clients to understand their recommendations and strategies and are happy to answer questions and educate their clients. Before you put a dime of your money with anyone, make sure you are comfortable with the financial adviser's professionalism and integrity.

Barrier #4

Business on a Handshake: The Trap of Informality

ost Latinos build their lives around informal relationships. We prefer to do business on a handshake rather than going through the bother of writing and signing contracts and agreements. When I first started looking at the beliefs that shape our relationship to money, I thought, Oh, this is just because we're a trusting people. But I've come to believe there's more to it than that. There are four reasons we prefer to do business on a handshake.

First, *we're not trusting: we're loyal.* Like almost everyone, we prefer to do business with people we know. We value our families and our community. We want to give our business to those around us, whether or not that's the best thing to do. And we believe that if we know someone—if they're a relative, or they've been recommended by a friend, or they've had a business down the street from us for years—we should be able to settle almost anything on the basis of a handshake.

Second, like people of many different ethnicities, *Latinos are intimidated by the legal language of contracts and written agreements.* For example, most of us have mutual funds as part of our retirement plans, but did you actually read the prospectuses of the funds you're invested in? If you've ever purchased a property and it's gone to escrow, here in California there are about 30 pages of documents filled with legal and financial language. As the buyer you're supposed to sign and initial almost every page. Well, no one is going to sit there and read it, much less understand it, unless they're lawyers or financial professionals themselves!

Third, *there is an enormous lack of financial education in the Latino community.* Approximately 6 out of 10 kids in East L.A. drop out of high school, and that doesn't include the kids who don't finish junior high. Even many of the kids who do start college don't finish. Instead, they get a job and start working to help out their families. When they do pull in a paycheck, do they open a bank account? No. Many Latinos prefer to use cash. They get their paycheck, go to the check-cashing service, take the money, and buy everything cash. So, unfortunately, they don't establish a credit record, which would get them used to dealing with credit responsibly and get them lower interest rates when they do have to borrow money to buy things like cars and houses.

Fourth, *many Latinos* (especially those who immigrated to the United States and have Spanish as their primary language) *have poor English skills.* Some of my clients are just getting comfortable with using English instead of Spanish. When they are faced with a contract in English, they believe there's no way they will ever understand it. Is it any wonder that so many Latinos give up and say to the salesperson or adviser, "I trust you. Let's shake on this and forget the contract, okay?"

Why do people allow themselves to be caught in the trap of informality? *Vergüenza*—embarrassment. Most people don't want to ask questions because they don't want to look stupid. Then, if they get themselves into a bad situation, they're too embarrassed to admit it. They won't try to get out of a bad contract, or even report the offender to an organization like the Better Business Bureau. They'd rather be ripped off than be embarrassed. And as a result, they keep getting ripped off again and again.

Informality: A Problem for Both Customers and Lenders

There are two huge problems with doing business on a handshake. The first is for the customer. I've seen so many people (Anglos as well as Latinos) who watch TV, see a great deal on a car or a mortgage or a credit card, and then end up with a loan where they're paying up to 29.9 percent, simply because they were too intimidated to read the contract. People walk into a dealership or an insurance office or even a bank and they see someone with a suit and tie on, a person who looks like a professional. They think, this person must know what he is doing; he will help me make the best decision. Unfortunately, the person with the suit is usually looking out for his or her best interests rather than the customer's. That's when customers end up with exorbitant loan or interest rates, unneeded insurance policies, and inappropriate investments.

I'll give you an example. I often tell clients to go to their bank and open a money market account, to take the place of a non-interest-bearing checking account. I've had some clients come back and tell me, "The bank officer opened the money market account for me, and guess what? He set up an annuity for me, too! He told me I could fund the money market through the annuity." The bank officer didn't tell the clients he received a commission on the annuity sale. The clients didn't need or want an annuity, but because the bank officer recommended it—and he was a professional—they signed on the dotted line.

The second problem actually occurs for the person who is offering the contract. In the Catholic church there are two kinds of sins: sins of commission and sins of omission. In contracts, the sins of omission are often the ones that come back to haunt you. As a customer, if a condition you think you agreed on isn't in the contract, it's too bad for you. Conversely, if you as a businessperson think you have an oral agreement with a customer, only to find out the customer thought you agreed on something different, you're the one who's out of luck. There is a *dicho*: "*No mas se acuerda de lo que le conviene*," meaning people only remember what they want to remember. No one ever remembers exactly what is said. They have their own version of what happened, and most likely it will be different from anyone else's. When you do business on a handshake, if there's a disagreement down the line, you're stuck in a "he said, I said" situation, and the entire arrangement can fall apart. As a businessperson, if you fail to get everything in writing, you're being irresponsible. As a customer, if you fail to get everything in writing, you're being irresponsible *and* naïve.

Lack of written agreements creates the most dissension when lending money to a family member or cosigning a loan. I always tell my clients, "Lending money to family members changes the relationship. Even though I know you're doing it because you want to help, all you'll end up with is bad feelings. Don't do it. If you want to transfer money to a family member, you're better off making it a gift rather than a loan." Cosigning a loan for someone is even worse, because now you are taking on an additional financial responsibility that you don't even benefit from! There's a reason that in the book of Proverbs it says, don't cosign a loan. More often than not when you cosign a loan, you're going to be stuck paying it off yourself.

We have to stop being intimidated by written agreements. In fact, we need to learn to *insist* on them. If it isn't written, it isn't real. Even if it's a few lines written on a scrap of paper saying, "On such-and-such a date, I will pay my cousin Sancho Ruiz $5,000 for his car, a Ford Escort," that scrap of paper can save you and Sancho a lot of grief in the long run. And if there's something we don't understand in any contract, we need to ask for explanations. And we must *never* sign anything until we are absolutely clear about what is said in the contract, what the terms are, and what we are agreeing to do.

What to Do When Faced with a Contract

All of us at one time or another will have some sort of contract stuck under our noses and be told, "Sign here." It could be an application for a loan or a credit card; it could be a promissory note, or a lease for our first apartment, or an agreement to buy our first house. It could be a contract for a gym membership or an employment application. Most people scan the paper, try to understand as much of it as possible, and then sign it immediately, hoping that everything is okay. That's a sure recipe for financial hardship. We have to understand that contracts are for our protection as much as for the other person's. If we master a few simple elements and, most important, are willing to ask questions, then contracts can be a powerful tool that will help us ensure a better financial future. Here are three things to keep in mind when dealing with contracts.

▶ **You must believe this is something you can learn and understand.**

Most people are intimidated by contracts. They hate dealing with legal and financial terms because they don't understand them. It's like being in a foreign country and not speaking the language—only in this case, not speaking the language can cost you a lot. But most Latinos have experience learning a new language. They know it can be difficult at first, but after a very short time the new language becomes much easier. Contracts are written in a new language, but once you understand a few key words, you can comprehend the meaning with a lot more confidence. However, if you look at a contract and tell yourself, "I'll never understand this," you're right. You've got to start with beliefs like, "I can learn this. I'm committed to mastering this because it is important. I'll do whatever it takes to get to the point where I can sign this with confidence that I understand what I'm agreeing to." With that attitude, a contract becomes an opportunity to be seized rather than an obstacle to be overcome.

▶ **Own your power: It's your money/time/decision.**

Even though it may not always seem so, as the client you ultimately have the power in the interaction. You're the one who
is going to spend the money for the car or the house or furniture or any other purpose. You're the one who will be responsible for paying the money back if you're applying for a loan. If
it's an employment application or contract, you're the one
who will be deciding to take the job and do the work. However,
when dealing with contracts most of us feel the other side has
power and smarts and we don't. That's a lie. A contract is an
agreement reached between two people/entities/institutions.
Your side has just as much clout as theirs does if you will step
up and take it. You have the right—indeed, the responsibility—to understand the terms of the agreement before you sign
anything. If you don't feel comfortable, you also have the right
to walk away without signing. Be warned, however: Once you
sign a contract, you have usually lost your right to walk away
unless there is a provision in the contract that allows you to do
so. That's another good reason never to sign any document
until you read and understand it first.

▶ **Be willing to admit what you know and what you don't
know.**

When dealing with contracts, the worst thing you can do is to
pretend you understand something when you don't. As I said
earlier, most people get lost in the financial and legal termi-
nology used in contracts; it can seem that contracts are written
deliberately to confuse us. In the case of dishonest business-
people, this can be true. But most contracts are written so as to

cover a lot of technicalities that may never occur but need to be addressed just in case.

Your job is to make sure you understand the basic points of the contract. Ask the other person to explain the provisions of the contract to you. Get the outline of the provisions in writing; that way you'll be able to refer to them later. Don't allow yourself to be pressured into signing something right away to "lock in" the deal. No really good deal will vanish in the time you take to review a contract. If it does, it wasn't a good deal to begin with. I've seen far too many people who sign contracts thinking they're getting a great deal on a car or a home or furniture, only to find out they have agreed to horribly high interest rates or thousands of dollars in extra fees. No respectable businessperson will balk at letting you review a contract for at least 24 hours. Stand your ground and insist upon having the time to review the contract thoroughly.

When reviewing the contract, make a list of any terms or provisions you don't understand, and ask for an explanation. Take notes, and let the other person see you writing things down. The written word is very powerful, and any notes you take will help if there is any disagreement. If you like, have someone else go with you when you review the contract. For my clients who don't read English well, I recommend they have someone else read the contract to them and explain unfamiliar terms. I also recommend that if it's an important contract, they have a professional, like an attorney, review it for them. Again, make sure the professional explains the terms of the contract to you. The goal is not for your attorney or adviser to say, "Fine," and for you to sign just because you trust them. The goal is for you to understand what you are agreeing to. Knowledge is power. The more you know, the easier it will be for you to understand other contracts in the future.

When to Say Yes—and No

As I said earlier, many Latinos start out by operating on a "cash only" basis. They cash their paychecks at the local check-cashing service and pay all their bills with cash. This is a pretty good strategy for making sure you don't live beyond your means. But in the United States, to get beyond subsistence-level living you need to establish a good credit record. And the only way to establish credit, strangely enough, is to learn to handle debt. That usually means signing some kind of contract—for a credit card, a car loan, a mortgage, and so on. So it's important to understand the basics of managing credit.

First and most obvious, *never borrow more than your current earnings will allow you to repay in a reasonable amount of time.* Especially in the last few years, credit card companies were issuing cards with ridiculously high credit limits on them. People would get the cards, think to themselves, Wow! A $10,000 limit! Now I can buy the furniture, go on vacation, and treat my family to some really nice gifts. They would forget that they were making $30,000 a year and spending $28,000 on food, shelter, transportation, taxes, and so on. When the bill for that $10,000 came in, they'd keep making the minimum payment—but most of the minimum payment was interest. The $10,000 principal wouldn't go down at all. And instead of saving for the future, these people would be paying off credit card bills for years and years.

The goal of establishing credit is to have access to it when you need it—for big purchases like cars and homes. It's also useful to have access to credit for emergencies (although if you are following a monthly savings plan, you should have some cash set aside for that). Credit is not to be used for impulse purchases or to get things you can't really afford. Think of credit as a test or an allowance: a way of using a relatively small amount of money to learn big lessons and to prove to the financial establishment that you can be trusted to handle money responsibly.

Second, *look at the total amount of debt, not the monthly payment.* I especially see people run into trouble with this when they are buying a car. A young couple walks into the dealership looking for a good, used, family car for about $10,000. The salesperson shows them an almost-new SUV and says, "You can have this for exactly the same monthly payment as you would for that 4-year-old station wagon you were looking at." However, the salesperson doesn't point out that the SUV will cost them over $21,000 including interest, and instead of paying off the station wagon in 3 years, the couple will be paying for the SUV for 6 years. Plus, every debt we incur is noted on what's called a credit report. These are the financial records on each of us that are kept by big credit bureaus. The more debt you have in proportion to your income, the less likely you are to be able to borrow any more money. If this young couple wants to buy a house, for example, that big auto loan might count against them and make it harder for them to get a mortgage.

The third basic to managing credit is to *pay your bills on time, every time.* I've seen too many Latinos (as well as Anglos) who say, "Honey, don't send in the payment this month, but send a double payment next month." That version of *mañana* thinking (see Barrier #9) can really hurt your credit record. Every late payment on a bill gets noted and counts against you when the credit bureaus evaluate your creditworthiness. Nowadays many credit card companies and lending institutions are charging very high fees for late payments. If you have a problem remembering to pay bills, some banks will allow you to pay by telephone or set up automatic bill paying through your checking account. Whatever strategy you use, paying your bills on time every time will help you keep your credit record clean and strong.

Fourth and last, *protect your creditworthiness*. Check your credit record regularly. You can do this by writing to some of the main credit bureaus like Equifax and requesting a copy of your credit record. People make mistakes, but so do banks, credit card companies, and merchants. If you find a mistake on your credit record, take it up with the bank or store that made the mistake. You can also file a protest with the credit bureau or have them put a note in your file explaining the incident. And never allow others to use your credit. This means your credit cards, bank account numbers, Social Security number, and so on. Your credit record is like your reputation: It's one of the most valuable things you possess, but once it's damaged, you can spend a lifetime cleaning it up. Put an effort into protecting your credit record from the start, and you'll find your road to financial greatness will be much smoother.

What should you do when you look at a contract or offer of credit and decide you don't want it? Or if, having said yes, you discover you've been cheated? The worst thing you can do is to let *vergüenza*, embarrassment, keep you from doing what's right.

It can be very tough to walk away when you've spent several hours at a dealership haggling over a car. But if the deal isn't right, the car won't be right either. Don't let yourself be pressured emotionally into something that goes against your best interests. Remember, it's your money, and ultimately it's your decision. You have to be willing to stand your ground, say no, and walk away.

What's even more difficult than walking away is to admit when you've been ripped off. Because of *vergüenza*, far too many people keep quiet and never try to do anything about even the most unfair contracts. However, the worst thing you can do is to keep quiet. You're not the first person to be taken advantage of, and you won't be the last—especially if you don't warn others by letting them know what happened to you! If you believe you have been cheated or treated unfairly, go to a trusted adviser and ask what you should do. There are local, state, and federal organizations that oversee almost every kind of business and profession in this country, and they all have formal complaint programs. If the issue is important enough, you may wish to consult an attorney to see if you have any legal redress, either through small claims or other civil courts. But don't let yourself be ripped off without a fight. Know your rights, get them in writing, and then hold yourself and the other parties to a contract that is fair to you both.

Traveling the road to financial greatness can be easy or hard, long or short. But your journey will be smoother if you know the rules of the road and follow them. Learning about contracts and credit is like studying the manual for the driver's license test. You may never need everything in the manual, but you darn well better know it just in case! And many of the lessons—which side to drive on, what red and green lights mean, how long it takes your car to stop—will become second nature as you get better and better at driving. As you begin to learn about contracts, when you get your first credit card or car loan or mortgage, you're learning "rules of the road" you will use again and again. Learn them well, and your trip to financial greatness will be very pleasant indeed.

Barrier #5

Machismo: *More Ego Can Mean Less Money*

achismo is a word that's seen as a hallmark of Latino culture, but I've found it operates in almost every culture in the world. In any society, usually it's the man who's seen as the one responsible for supporting his family. Even today, how many men do you see in the United States who stay home to take care of the kids and the household while the woman works? And most families (not just Latinos) connect the man's responsibility for providing for his family to his overall responsibility for the family finances.

But *machismo* can harm a man in the area of financial dealings by creating what I call *financial blind spots*. Some Latino men won't admit they don't know everything about finances, and so they'll plunge into a business deal without the critical information that would make the difference between earning and losing money. And once they've made a bad decision—signed a contract at 25 percent interest, for example, or given money to someone only to have that person vanish—*machismo* won't let them admit they made a mistake. They don't want anybody to find out they were taken, so instead of being upset and doing something about the mistake, they stay quiet and just let it go. And then the criminals who are preying on our communities just keep on doing it, because no one's speaking up to stop them.

Machismo affects Latino men from a very early age. It determines their life path, their choices in education, career, mates, and so on. Many Latinos, for example, don't go to college because they believe a man is supposed to go to work and start supporting himself and a family as quickly as possible. They don't get the education in finances, contracts, and money. Instead, they're earning a living from a very young age. Nowadays, you'll often find more Latinas in college than Latinos! But when a Latina gets married, even if she has more education than her husband does, what typically happens? As a financial adviser, I can tell you that the woman will usually transfer her accounts to her husband's bank, and from then on the husband will control the money. It has nothing to do with competence or who has more money; it's accepted by both Latinos and Latinas that the man is in charge of the money the family earns. I've even had clients who ask me to prepare their taxes, and then right in front of me they sign their wife's name to their joint tax return. "She doesn't need to see this—I handle all the finances," they tell me.

The Effects of *Machismo*

The effects of *machismo* are widespread and sometimes conflicting. For example, some Latino men get jealous when their wives
earn more money than they do. Even though it may mean financial hardship, husbands will pressure wives to quit their jobs and
stay home to take care of the kids. Also, a lot of men who get in
trouble financially never tell their wives. Or they tell their wives
when it is too late, and then the women have to cope with the
financial mess.

Machismo also affects the way men make decisions about how
and where to spend money. I was speaking to a woman friend of
mine the other day, and she said, "I've noticed that Latino men
tend to make big financial decisions on their own. Even when the
decision will have a major impact on the family, they decide first
and then let their wives know about it. Men will come home and
say, 'Guess, what, honey? I just bought a car!' Whereas women
tend to make joint decisions: they want to discuss things before
moving forward." In most families, joint decision making creates
far fewer problems and less conflict. But a lot of men feel it's not
masculine to involve their wives in such things. "After all, I
earned the money—I have the right to spend it how I want,"
they'll say.

Machismo based on ego and false pride can cause men to act
selfishly when it comes to money. They stop looking at the big
picture and don't take into account the needs of the family.
They'll buy a new car simply because they want one, forgetting
that the payments will put an enormous strain on the family
finances. Or they'll put all their money into a risky investment

without considering the people who will be the most directly affected by a financial loss—their wives and children.

This attitude of "my way or the highway" definitely causes problems. Today Latinas are more willing to stand on their own because they can, and they're less likely to put up with a man who won't let them control at least part of the household money. Even if the Latina agrees that the husband should earn the money and handle the finances, she often has a far better grasp of just where the money goes than her husband does. In fact, most men don't want to know about the details of budgeting and running the household; they leave that to their wives. As a result, Latinas are often very realistic when it comes to money. They know how much it costs to run the household, and when their husbands make big financial decisions that could potentially put the family income in jeopardy, it can cause a lot of upset.

I tell my clients and the people in my seminars that the journey to financial greatness requires both husband and wife to be involved and educated about their money. "The manliest thing you can do is to handle your money well," I tell men. "And since the average man will die before his wife does, it is important that women become competent about money. So you take the lead." The best way for a man to provide for his family is by mastering finances and then involving his family, especially his wife, in the financial decision-making process. After all, if a man wants his wife to respect him, then he needs to respect her. A real man is confident enough in himself to let others know about his finances and to let them have a say in where the family money goes. The more a man involves the rest of his family in financial decisions, the happier everyone is. Give and you'll get back. Sow the seeds and you'll reap a lot of benefit by keeping everyone involved.

Latinas and *Machisma*:
An Equal-Opportunity Trap

Unfortunately, as Latinas move into the workforce, becoming single heads of households, and taking charge of their own finances, they are falling into some of the same traps as Latino men. I've seen the problems of *machisma* in some of my most successful Latina clients. While Latinas may have more experience in the kind of day-to-day budgeting needed to stretch a paycheck, they also may have more trouble making the big decisions about money—buying a house, for example, or signing a contract for a car purchase. And just like Latinos, Latinas are reluctant to admit when they don't know about or understand complicated financial dealings. So Latinas can fall into the same kind of traps as men: signing bad contracts and then hiding their mistakes because they don't want to appear stupid or helpless.

I had one young woman come into my office and consult me about some tax planning. I looked over her retirement portfolio and noticed she had a rather expensive annuity policy. When I asked her about it, she got very defensive. "I bought it 5 years ago, right after I got my divorce," she said. "The man at my bank said it would provide me with guaranteed income when I retire." I pointed out to her that she was still in her early thirties—a long way from retirement—and the money she was paying for that annuity every month probably could be invested in her 401(k) that would provide her with greater returns and a larger nest egg when she did reach 65. "That's what my other tax planner told me," she replied stubbornly. "But I can't go back to the bank and tell them I made a mistake. I'd look like an idiot." This woman was prepared to take a financial hit totaling tens of thousands of dollars over the course of her life just because she didn't want to look like an idiot in front of a financial services salesperson! That's *machisma* at its most destructive.

Pride, ignorance, and stubbornness are equal-opportunity stumbling blocks on the journey to financial greatness. Don't let *machismo* or *machisma* get in your way. Be willing to ask questions and admit mistakes. It's better to admit you're wrong and start doing the right thing than keep doing the wrong thing and expect the right result.

Are You Letting *Vergüenza* Hold You Back?

One day in the fall of 2001, Roberto, a good friend I have known for years, came to see me to talk about his finances. Although he is a successful attorney, Roberto confided that he finally had come to terms with himself and decided that he needed my help. He was ashamed and embarrassed to admit that even though he earns a lot of money, he had no savings, no estate plan, no money saved for his daughter's education, and very little in retirement funds. He said that the attack on the United States had shocked him into doing something. But confessing his financial state of affairs to me was the most difficult thing he had ever done. He told me that he felt unbelievable shame, guilt, and embarrassment.

The sad part was that I also felt shame, guilt, and embarrassment. I had assumed that my friend was financially secure because of his status in the community. Roberto and I have known each other for over 10 years, and we have gone through many crises together. We have been there for each other through divorce, family deaths, and other tragedies, and shared many good times as well. Roberto knew I was a professional financial adviser, yet he didn't want me to know about his personal finances because it was something that he considered very private. (One of the biggest taboos left in our society is the discussion of money.) Unfortunately, the economic downturn had affected his law practice so much that he was afraid of losing his home. His clients were having a difficult time paying him, and he hadn't brought home a decent paycheck in several weeks.

Roberto is not unlike many Latinos who live paycheck to paycheck. If the average Latino became unemployed, he or she would be approximately three months away from being homeless. Yet far too many Latino men let *machismo* and its related emotions—ego, false pride, selfishness, stubbornness—get in the way of their seeking help. "It's not manly," they say. "I'll get myself out of this somehow." However, I believe that *machismo* actually makes us *less* manly. In fact, it can turn us into financial wimps. Wimps sit there and do nothing. They react to what is happening in negative ways and then worry about what they can't control. Financial wimps would rather watch their families do without the basics of life than admit they've made mistakes or need help with their finances.

But I also believe *real* men want to be heroes instead of wimps. Heroes make things happen. They are proactive. They can admit their mistakes and change for the better. They are willing to put false pride aside and ask for help if they need it. They put the good of their families ahead of any selfish desires on their part.

They do the things that they can control, and they are manly enough to include their families in important decisions. They save for emergencies and take care of themselves so they can take care of their families. Heroes don't use finances as a measure of their worth as men. Instead, they recognize that money is simply a means to an end, a way of creating security and abundance for the people who are important to them. I am very proud of my friend Roberto because he found the courage to stop being a slave to false *machismo* and the fear of *vergüenza*. He became a financial hero to himself and his family. And I believe he is a great role model for all of us as we travel the road to financial greatness.

Barrier #6

Don't Be a Crab: Scarcity and Abundance

O nce there was a man who had been fishing all day, and he caught three buckets of crabs— German crabs, French crabs, and Mexican crabs. On the docks he met a friend he hadn't seen for a while, so they chatted. The friend looked over the fisherman's shoulder and noticed that while two of the three buckets of crabs were covered, the third was not. "Hey, *amigo!*" he said to the fisherman. "The crabs are trying to climb out of your basket. You'd better cover it up like the other two." The fisherman said, "Nah—those are the Mexican crabs. As soon as one climbs up the side of the basket, the others pull it back down."

When I tell this story in my seminars, there's a lot of knowing laughter in the room. It's a sad but true commentary on the Latino community, and it represents a belief that holds us back. As soon as someone in our community attains some level of success, it seems to be almost an automatic response to try to shame that person into believing that they are getting above themselves. If you move to a better neighborhood, your old neighbors will tell you, *"Que se te va subir a la cabeza,"* which means, "You are going to get a big head." When you buy anything nice, you constantly hear, *"¿Como te crees?"* "Who do you think you are?" A Latino comedian tells a story about buying a car after he did his first television role. He bought a brand-new Honda Accord and proudly drove it to his parents' house. Did his relatives say, "Congratulations—nice car!"? Of course not. They said, "You think you're better than us? You're not going to talk to us anymore because we drive old cars?" Successful Latinos tell me that often their own families and communities make them feel guilty for doing well. It's as if we believe the old saying, "Misery loves company."

A friend of mine drives a nice but not overly flashy BMW. If people saw him driving down the street in Newport Beach, California (where I used to work), they would think he was a stockbroker, banker, or entrepreneur. But here in East L.A., people see the car and think this young man is a drug dealer or a moneylender out to cheat his clients. They can't believe that anyone could come by the money for that kind of car honestly. *"Como se cree,"* Who does he think he is, driving a BMW in the barrio? That kind of attitude in our community can keep us from taking full advantage of the financial opportunities open to us. When we see a young Latina making it in business, we think, why does she have so much money? She must be doing something wrong, instead of saying to ourselves, It's great that she is so successful. Let me find out what she's doing and maybe I can be successful, too!

The "Tall Poppy" Syndrome

In my profession, I see a lot of successful people whom I call "firsts." They're the first in their family to go to college, the first in the community to become a district attorney or scientist or Internet entrepreneur or university professor, the first of their peers to run a manufacturing company. They should be proud of who they are and what they've accomplished, yet all too often, they find that their friends and family members are alienated by their success. It seems that other Latinos are going out of their way to slam doors in their faces. In Australia they call it the tall poppy syndrome: as soon as one person sticks his head up above the others, he is immediately chopped down. People feel threatened by others' success if they themselves don't feel successful. These successful individuals feel they're being judged by their own community. As a financial planner, one of the advantages I have with my Latino clients is that I don't judge them. For the first time in their lives they can share their dreams with someone who believes in them, too. Many people are afraid to talk about their dreams because their families make them feel they're crazy to have such high aspirations or goals. But if you keep your dreams to yourself, all too often they stay dreams. Sharing them with others helps you believe in your dreams as well as yourself. But if our young people don't feel that their families and community will support their dreams, how much poorer does that make all of us?

While successful people may feel guilt about their success, the kind of negative emotions expressed by their families and the community are worse. Negative emotions like envy, anger, jealousy bring out the worst in us. They limit us; they contract rather than expand our thinking. Remember those crabs in the story? Their entire world is the little bucket they're stuck in. And they're so busy making sure that none of the other crabs reach a higher position in the bucket, they're guaranteeing that all of them are going to be on somebody's dinner plate in a very short time!

Negative emotions like envy and jealousy keep us from tapping into the kind of expansion and abundance we truly desire. I also believe in the old expression, "What goes around comes around." When we see someone who is successful and think bad things about them, what does that say about our own beliefs about success? And if we believe that success means we're going to be hated by our friends, family, and community, how likely are we to succeed?

Scarcity and Abundance: The Pie Fallacy

At the core of the beliefs that make us jealous or envious of someone else's success are our feelings about scarcity and abundance. Scarcity means if you win, I lose. If you get more, someone else gets less. If someone opens a financial planning business across the hall from you, you're in trouble because there are only so many clients out there who need financial planning services. Scarcity thinking views life like a pie in a family of very hungry people. There's only so much pie to go around, and once the pie is gone, it's gone. If you take a big piece, then that means there's less for the rest of us. If you think of life like that, no wonder you get angry if you see someone who has more "pie" than you do, and do your best to make sure they don't take any more!

But I don't believe that's true. I believe in living in abundance, where if I win, you win, too. If I'm successful, it can open the doors for you to be successful as well. If you open a financial planning business across the hall, great! There are plenty of people who need our services, and two businesses in the same building means more traffic in the area and more potential clients. There's so much abundance in this world that there will always be enough for anyone who is willing to work for it.

In my belief—and this is the belief of every wealthy and successful person I have ever encountered—there's always enough pie to go around because there's always someone somewhere who's baking more. In truth, the smartest people never spend time worrying about who's got the biggest piece of pie because they're out there building more pie shops! We need to invest in ourselves and our businesses, bringing "pie shops" of all kinds into the Latino community. If you just make the pie bigger, you're still going to run out of pieces at some point because it's only one pie. And people will continue to think, "I gotta get my piece now. The heck with everyone else, this is all the pie there is and there ain't gonna be no more." But when we build pie shops, when we create business and abundance in our own communities, we can say to each other, "Be my guest: go ahead and eat the rest of that pie. I know there's another pie coming." When you believe there is always going to be more pie, then it doesn't matter if your brother-in-law buys a Mercedes, or if a competitor opens an office in your neighborhood, or if your daughter moves into a house that's larger than yours. You know that you can have your piece of the pie, too, if you're willing to work for it. There will be plenty of pie to go around.

The Secret to Abundance: Gratitude

If you find yourself "buying into" feelings of scarcity, envy, and jealousy, there are three simple ways to turn yourself around. First, be aware of what those feelings are doing to you as well as the people you're jealous of. Do you *like* feeling envious or jealous or worrying that you won't get your share? Probably not. Can you choose another way to feel? Absolutely. And that's the second secret: Choose to feel good about the success of others. What if you were sincerely able to congratulate someone who's doing well? Instead of feeling threatened, what if you could regard her as a door opener for your success? If what goes around comes around, what can you do for them that you hope someone will do for you when you're in that position? I'm a big believer in mentors and role models: I want to learn from the best people who have succeeded in different areas of their lives. What if every person who succeeded had something to teach you that will make it easier for you to succeed? If you're able to change your attitudes, how much more likely are you to want to succeed when it's your turn?

The third and most powerful way to open yourself up to abundance and success is gratitude. Be grateful for what you have. Instead of looking at someone else and saying, "Why aren't I that successful?" take a moment to appreciate the gifts you already possess. I was reading a story the other day about a man who was complaining to his brother about his weight. "Look at my friend Ramon!" he said. "Ramon has a great body and he barely works at it. I have to drag myself to the gym every day to lose even a little weight, and as soon as I stop going, I put on 5 pounds. I hate going to the gym! Why can't I be like Ramon?" His brother looked at the man with anger and disgust. "Don't you *ever* complain to me about having to go to the gym!" he said, and he lifted up his hand a fraction of an inch and brought it down—on the arm of his wheelchair. The man's brother was a quadriplegic.

We sometimes get so wrapped up in looking at what we don't have that we forget the amazing gifts we have already received. Life. Health. Family. Whatever level of abundance we enjoy. Gratitude is the ultimate secret of success. Whenever I start feeling pressured or sorry for myself, I think, "Man, I've got a good income, a great business, a wonderful wife, great kids; I'm lucky and blessed. I've worked really hard for this, but I've got a lot to be grateful for." Gratitude is the antidote to scarcity thinking. And it's easy! Just find something you can be grateful for in the moment: if nothing else, be grateful that you're still breathing.

When we focus on gratitude and abundance, when we believe there's more than enough to go around, when instead of being envious and jealous of the success of others we regard their success as a pathway we can follow in our own pursuit of financial greatness, then we stop being crabs and start being fishermen in charge of creating our own abundance. All it takes is a little skill, a little patience, a little hard work—and a hook baited with the belief that we are ready to make our own success.

Barrier #7

Fatalism: A Divine Excuse for Doing Nothing

There is a saying in Spanish, "*Si Dios quiere,*" which means, "God willing." I hear this all the time. For example, I'll call clients to schedule an appointment to go over their financial plan. I'll say, "Okay, I'll see you on Tuesday at three o'clock in the afternoon," and the most common answer I hear is, "*Si Dios quiere.*" God willing. "God wants what is best for us," I tell them. "God will help you, but you have to help yourself." But what's the answer again? "*Si Dios quiere.* It's not in my control, it's in God's control."

Too many of my clients remind me of the man who lived in a house right next to a river. It had been raining steadily for about a week, and Juan noticed that the river water was rising and starting to flood his backyard. That afternoon the local sheriff arrived in a patrol car. "Juan, you'd better get out of here," he said. "We've had warnings from upstream that a big flood is on its way. Let me take you to higher ground."

"No, thank you," Juan replied. "I have faith in God. I will pray to Him to protect me."

The sheriff shrugged, got in his car, and drove away. The rain kept falling and the water in the river kept rising until it covered the foundation of Juan's house. The next morning the water was up to his front door. As Juan looked out of his house at the water all around him, he saw his neighbor, Pedro, rowing toward him in a small boat. "Get in, Juan!" Pedro urged. "The water's still rising. Your house is going to be swept away. Come with me and you'll be safe."

Juan shook his head. "God will rescue me," he said. Pedro argued with him for a long time, but in the end he gave up and rowed away.

That night an emergency services helicopter was flying along the course of the river, looking for stranded or drowning people. As their searchlight swept over the roof of Juan's house, they could see him clinging to the chimney. Water was lapping at his feet; in no more than an hour, the entire house would be covered. Quickly the men in the helicopter lowered a rope.

"Grab hold and we'll pull you up!" they said to Juan.

"No!" Juan cried, his eyes tightly closed. "I have faith. God will rescue me!"

Just then the helicopter got a call to help someone who was drowning a short distance away. When they flew back over Juan's house an hour later, the water had risen past the level of the chimney. Juan was nowhere to be seen. He had drowned.

When Juan reached heaven, he was pretty upset. He stormed through the pearly gates and straight up to God. "What happened?" Juan shouted. "I prayed ceaselessly for you to save me. I had faith in you, and you failed me."

"My son," God replied. "I sent you a car, a boat, and a helicopter, but you didn't take any of them. What more do you want?"

This kind of fatalistic attitude—that things will only happen if God wants them to, and we're not responsible—stops many of us from taking the actions that will help us achieve sound financial futures. If we believe it's up to God to take care of everything, where's the incentive to take action on our own? Sometimes people won't do anything to change their financial situation because they think, "If I'm poor I was meant to be poor. It's God's will." They find consolation for having to do without because they believe nothing would change their fate.

The strain of fatalism that runs through Latino culture is insidious yet extremely damaging. You hear this kind of attitude in other expressions. *"Lo que sera, sera,"* what will be, will be. The Arabs (who were a major influence on Spanish culture as far back as the 8th century AD) say, *"Insh'allah,"* which shows up in Spanish as *"Ojala"* and means "Would to God." It means you're hoping that something will happen. But it rarely means that you're taking any affirmative steps to *make* things happen.

I remind my clients in almost every session: "God makes the fish and God makes the nets, but God doesn't put fish *in* the nets. God helps those who help themselves." Then I tell a story about a man traveling through the middle of a desert. He's walked for hours without seeing a trace of green. Then all of a sudden, he comes upon a wall. He follows the wall to a gate, through which he can see a magnificent house surrounded by green lawns and a beautiful garden filled with flowers and fruit trees. The traveler also sees a man in the garden watering a hibiscus bush.

"May I come inside?" asks the traveler.

"Certainly," said the man with the watering can. "This is my home. Feel free to come in and rest from your journey."

After giving the traveler a cool drink, the owner of the home takes him on a tour of the garden. The traveler marvels at how green and beautiful everything is. Turning to the owner, he says, "You are so lucky. God has truly blessed you."

The owner smiles. "To be honest, God gave me the land, but I had to *work* for all this!"

I believe God wills that we make the most of our hard-earned money to create financial greatness for ourselves and our families. And that means taking charge of our finances, being responsible enough to learn how to make our money work for us in as many ways as possible. Like the man in the story, God's will for us may be to have a beautiful house and magnificent gardens—but we usually have to put in the work along the way ourselves.

Barrier #8

The Lotto Mentality: Getting Something for Doing Nothing

Not too far from my office, there's a convenience store where I occasionally stop for a paper or a cup of coffee. One afternoon I walked by and noticed a long line in front of the counter. "What's going on?" I asked a woman in line. "Don't you know?" she asked excitedly. "The California Super Lotto jackpot is up to $79 million this week. I'm buying tickets for my whole family. We're going to be rich!"

This attitude of getting something for nothing has been an extremely destructive force in the Latino community. Often we seem to believe that we can get things without having to work for them. The belief isn't one of entitlement: Latinos are hard workers, and we don't believe anyone owes us anything. But we're not above looking for shortcuts on the road to success. And taking shortcuts has consequences. It's just like cramming for an exam—you study just enough to pass the test but you never really learn the material. In fact, you forget almost everything as soon as the test is over. You lose any benefit that you may have gained if you had actually learned what the course had to teach. I call this willingness to look for shortcuts the "lotto mentality," and I believe it is nothing more than a lowering of our personal standards and ethics.

There are two words in common use among Latinos that describe this "getting something for nothing" attitude. First is *chapuceria*, which means "sloppy." It means putting something together as quickly as possible, without any concern for the quality of the job or how long it will last. Cramming for an exam is a *chapuceria*. Putting on a roof by slapping shingles on top of the house, not caring whether the roof will leak when it rains, is a *chapuceria*. Building a house without digging a proper foundation first is a *chapuceria*. And expecting to finance your retirement by winning the lotto is definitely a *chapuceria*. It's a sloppy way to prepare for your golden years. In fact, it's almost certain not to work, as you're more likely to get struck by lightning than you are to win a sizable sum in the lottery.

The second word that I associate with the lotto mentality is *movidas*, which literally means "moves," but in the Latino community has come to mean "scam." What's your *movida?* What's your racket, your angle, your scam? How can you figure out a way to get something for nothing? "Hey, my brother works at this restaurant on Tuesday night from 7 to 9. Let's go then so we can get some free drinks." "Hey, my sister gave me a hot stock tip. She heard about it from someone at her church who works for this company that's being taken over. If you buy this, you'll make a killing." "Hey, I've got an uncle who can tile your kitchen floor, but it'll take 5 years because he sneaks three tiles at a time out of

Home Depot." "You need your house rewired? My brother knows how to do it—he's not a licensed contractor though." Of course, when your house burns down because of the brother's shoddy work, you're stuck. Everyone is so focused on outfoxing the system and getting something for nothing, we forget that we're usually the ones who suffer in the end from our lack of integrity and low standards.

If you want to do or build something worthwhile or good, you have to be willing to put in the time and work needed and use the best tools available. Imagine what would happen if a farmer decided he or she could take a few shortcuts when it came to the crops. "I don't need to plant in the spring. I can wait until summer and still have enough of a harvest in the fall." "I don't need to fertilize and weed; the plants can take care of themselves." "I don't need to water every day; I'll try to get around to it once a week if I remember." There's an old saying: "You can't fool Mother Nature." I'd like to amend that and say, "You can't pull a *movida* on the laws of nature." What you plant, you're going to reap. How much time and effort you're willing to put into something will pay dividends. If you think you can get around putting in the work, in the short term you may be able to get away with it, but in the long run, *chapuceria*—sloppiness—will always come back to haunt you.

Easy Come, Easy Go

Even if you were to win the lottery, it won't be the solution to all your problems, simply because wealth that is won rather than earned never lasts. There are horror stories of people who won millions in the lottery and within a few years were dead broke or dead. Unless they already knew how to handle money, they'll either squander their winnings or get taken by unscrupulous villains eager to pull a *movida* on them.

The same thing can happen with people who inherit money or come into a trust fund. Some kids who know they're going to inherit a bundle will use the time until then to make their own money. They work hard at learning to be responsible stewards of wealth, and when the inheritance comes to them, they use it to increase their net worth. But other kids figure, "Why should I work? I'm going to inherit all this money someday. I'll just kick back until then." They never learn the true value of money because they never make the equation between effort and reward. As a result, when they come into their inheritance, they usually squander it. They didn't build the proper personality or character traits to do what's right.

At the bottom of the lotto mentality is greed, and greed causes people to make mistakes, take shortcuts, and often get suckered into all kinds of schemes and scams. I see this all the time in the Latino community. "My brother-in-law tells me he's got a real estate deal where we can triple our money overnight!" "I'm going to the casinos—I'll make a bundle on the slots!" "I saw a flier on a telephone pole saying I can make $5,000 stuffing envelopes for a few hours a night. I'll bet I can earn enough to buy a new car this year!" "My coworker wants me to work with her on this multilevel marketing business. She says I can earn up to $10,000 a month, and all I have to do is make a few phone calls!" As a financial professional, I've seen a million of these get-rich-quick schemes, and I've seen some of my clients get into serious financial trouble as a result.

There is no such thing as instant money. Some philosophers tell us that money is simply a symbol of the exchange of energy— the energy required to produce the goods we buy is exchanged for the effort we expended to earn the right to buy them. If this is true, then get-rich-quick schemes disturb that energy flow because we are putting out almost no energy and expecting to get an abundance of energy in return. Let's use multilevel marketing as an example. I respect those who are successful at multilevel marketing because I know how much work goes into establishing and maintaining that business. As a professional tax preparer and adviser for 17 years, however, I've also seen many more people who got into multilevel marketing thinking they could make a lot of money without doing much, only to find their financial rewards are absolutely equal to the effort they're willing to put in.

In life, effort equals reward. If by any chance your effort pays off all at once with a lot of reward—you get to the top of that multilevel network, or you sell a business you've built for the last 20 years, or you get promoted and all of a sudden you're making four times what you made last year—you've got to be prepared to handle the responsibility of abundance. Money doesn't "make" us: usually it just makes us more of who we already are. And quick money can test the character we have to its utmost. Only when we have a strong foundation of personal standards, morals, and ethics can we handle the demands and privileges of money in a way that will make us proud of who we are and what we can do.

The way to overcome the limiting belief of getting something for nothing starts with building a strong foundation for your life by taking personal accountability for yourself and the standards you choose. It's a known fact that when you build a house you need to put an 18- to 24-inch foundation under it. If you want to build a skyscraper, you need to sink the foundation several feet into the ground for the building to stay upright. It's the same with your personal foundation, which is made up of your work ethic, morals, and standards. How high you can build your life depends on how deep and strong your personal foundation is. If you were to choose a shack, or a house, or a mansion to represent you, what would you choose? And is your foundation deep and strong enough to support what you want to build?

A house built on a weak foundation will eventually fall, but a house built on a strong and deep foundation will withstand most catastrophes. When you dig deep to create a foundation of personal accountability, ethics, a willingness to put in the effort, and the unwillingness to cheat yourself by taking unethical shortcuts, then I believe you'll build a life you can look upon with pride. Instead of "easy come, easy go," your life will attract wealth because you will have earned it, and taken care of it, with integrity.

Barrier #9

The Mañana *Syndrome:*
The Pain of Procrastination

The stereotype of Latinos is that they respond to a request to get anything done with, "I'll do it *mañana*—tomorrow." But when I talk about the *mañana* syndrome, I mean something entirely different, something I call "the pain of procrastination." It means living only for today and not thinking or planning for tomorrow.

How many people in the United States today, including Latinos, live from paycheck to paycheck? How many people aren't planning for their financial future? All too often, I see clients who are concentrating on fulfilling their immediate needs without ever looking a few years down the road. I'll ask, "What about college for your kids? Your own retirement?" and they'll answer, "I can't start saving for that now. All my money is going toward my family's current needs. I'll look at putting money aside as soon as I get a raise," or "pay off the washing machine," or "get my business on its feet." To quote Stephen Covey, they're focusing on things that are urgent rather than keeping an eye on what's truly important.

There's nothing wrong with dealing with things that are urgent. The problem is that most of us never get around to the other things that are far more important when it comes to the ultimate quality of our lives. Like saving for retirement. Like spending time with our kids when they're growing up. Like keeping our relationships with our spouses strong. A self-improvement author once wrote about "Someday Isle," the island of unfulfilled dreams where procrastinators end up. It's called Someday Isle because everyone on it walks around saying, "Someday I'll . . ." "Someday I'll start my own business." "Someday I'll spend the weekend with my kids." "Someday I'll go on that second honeymoon." "Someday I'll put away money for retirement." But "someday" never comes, and all they have left are a bunch of empty promises and painful regrets.

Latinos are famous for living for the day and not planning for tomorrow. And I know that many people feel they are just barely keeping their heads above water dealing with the urgent stuff. "I have to get the car fixed," they'll tell me. "I can't put money away this month. I'll do it next month." Their intentions are always good—but you know where the road paved with good intentions leads. In fact, I once heard a pastor say, "If the devil doesn't make you bad, he makes you busy." In the busyness of life, we forget about the important stuff, like our future. I tell my clients, "To reach financial greatness, you have to have one eye on the present and one on the future at all times. Yes, handle the emergencies, but start preparing for the future, too. If you had prepared for the future by saving money all the months when your car didn't need to be fixed, wouldn't you have the money to fix it now *and* still be able to put money away?"

The "Why Bother?" Serenade

Another problem that arises with the *mañana* syndrome is what I call the "why bother" serenade, which is linked closely to fatalism (Barrier #7). I have so many friends and clients who come to me and say, "Why should I save for my child's college education? No one in my family has ever gone to college." Or, "Why should I send my daughter to college? All she's going to do is get married and have kids." Or even, "Why should I save for retirement? I'll get Social Security, and my kids will take care of any needs I have over and above what I get from the government." They see absolutely no reason to set aside money today for a future benefit they don't think they need.

But such people are in denial. Maybe nobody in the family has gone to college before, but nowadays even being a car mechanic or a plumber or almost any job that pays more than minimum wage requires some kind of advanced education or training. Yes, a daughter may go out and get married, but many Latinas are spending several years working before they have children. And even after the kids arrive, more and more Latinas are going back to work, earning incomes that provide a better life for their families. Yes, your kids may take care of you when you retire, and you may get a regular Social Security check. But Social Security was never designed to be a retiree's only means of support. It was always supposed to be supplemental to pensions or savings that the worker had accumulated. And by the way, have you looked at the cost of living lately? Social Security covers less and less of our basic needs for food and shelter. Wouldn't your retirement be a whole lot better if you could support yourself financially, whether you were living with your children or on your own?

We have to learn to develop the ant's mentality instead of the grasshopper's. You remember the tale of the ant and the grasshopper—how the grasshoppers played all summer long while the ants worked hard to fill the ant hill with food. When winter came, the grasshoppers shivered and starved, but the ants had plenty of food to eat. What if instead of storing up food, the ants had said, "Yeah, we know winter's coming, but that's life. Some of us will live, and some will die. It's always been that way. Why should we try to make it different?" There would have been a lot more ants dead than alive at the end of the winter. All of us know that we need to have money saved for the future, whether it be to take care of emergencies, cover our basic needs when we retire, or just to have a little "walking-around" money if we do live with our kids when we're old. But the time to put that money aside is now, not later—today, not *mañana*. Because *mañana* comes sooner than we think and costs a lot more than we want it to.

The Pain of Procrastination

In my seminars I do a simple exercise that helps people understand the pain of short-term thinking. I say, "Close your eyes for a moment. Now imagine you're 65, and you're retiring. You've worked hard all your life, and now you're ready to take it easy. But you never put any money aside for your retirement while you were working. You have about $500 in the bank. You wait eagerly to get your first Social Security check in the mail, but when you open it, you realize it will barely pay your rent. You have no money for groceries or gas. You have no choice—you have to move in with your son. He has his own wife and family, naturally, but they rearrange things so you have a place to live. You spend your retirement sharing a room with your grandson. Even though your son and his family love you, you feel you are a burden on them. You have no money, no freedom, no prospects. How does that feel? Is that the kind of future you want?"

By this point, the group is intensely uncomfortable—which is exactly what I want. It's important that we feel *emotionally* the consequences of our current shortsighted behavior. Once the people in my seminars get that experience, have them close their eyes again and imagine what life will be like if they retire having saved enough to support themselves in comfort. I get them to feel how great it will be to have those choices: the freedom to do what they want, provide for their kids rather than their kids providing for them, perhaps travel to see relatives and friends in other cities and countries. I show them how long-term thinking will help them create the future of their dreams starting right now.

You may think this exercise is pretty strong, but doesn't it seem that our lives unfold in just that way? We start work, blink, and all of a sudden we're getting our gold watch. We get married, and the next thing we know, kids appear. In another blink of an eye they're graduating, going off to college or work, and getting married themselves. The *mañana* we thought we had plenty of time to prepare for suddenly is next week, or next month, or even the next minute. As Stephen Covey states, "We must begin with the end in mind." I've always said you have to have a dual vision: one eye on the present, the other on the future. Ideally that works out better. We have the power to create whatever financial future we want, as long as we start taking charge of our finances today, not *mañana*.

How do we get past the tendency to live for today and put off thinking about tomorrow? We need to figure out how to make the important urgent. And the only way to do that is to take a look at the big picture. You'll learn a very simple process to get clear about your financial big picture in Part 2 of this book, but the first step is to decide *what* you are saving for and *why* it's important to you. As many self-improvement experts have said, "Once you have a big enough 'why,' you'll find out 'how' to get it."

One of the easiest ways to get past *mañana* thinking is to set up systems for saving that you don't even have to think about. Put your savings on automatic pilot. Sign up to have a certain amount deducted automatically from your paycheck and put into a savings account, money market, 401(k), IRA, or any other long-term investment. Instead of spending a year-end bonus or inheritance, invest the money in your future. Remember, however, automatic investing is kind of like using cruise control in a car: you still have to keep your eyes on the road and stay aware of changing financial conditions.

Above all, remember that our biggest ally in investing is the power of time. We make the most of our money when we invest small amounts now, and then allow the power of compounding to grow those small amounts into large ones through the years. If anything can illustrate for you the advantages of investing today instead of waiting until tomorrow, it's the power of compounding. Let me give you an example of what I mean. Say you started investing at the age of 20. Every day you put aside just $2: that's

$61 a month, and $730 a year. You put your $730 a year in investments that gave you an average 12 percent rate of return. You never put in any more than $2 a day but you never missed a day either. By the time you reached 65, you would have over *$1 million* saved for retirement!

Now, let's look at what happens if you wait 5 years to start investing. By age 25, you have to put in $3.57 a day, $109 a month, and $1,304 a year to have that same $1 million at age 65. And if you wait until you're 35, you'd have to invest $11.35 a day, $345 a month, and $4,144 a year to have that same $1 million! That's the power of compounding. The more time you have for your money to grow, the less money you need to produce results. The less time you have, the more money you'll need. By the way, if you waited until age 45 to start investing, you'd need $38.02 every day, $1,157 a month, and $13,879 a year, invested at 12 percent interest, to have that $1 million.

Procrastination is a thief that steals our financial future. Every day that we wait we lose a little more of the power of time to help us create a future of abundance rather than lack. That's how *mañana* thinking can steal our future. Let time be your ally, not a thief who silently takes your health and happiness. Instead of *mañana*, tomorrow, say *hoy*—today!

Barrier #10

Pobrecito Me: Conflicting Beliefs and Attitudes About Money

l dinero es raiz de toda clase de males. "Money is the root of all evil." How many times have we heard that and other negative beliefs about money? "Money leads to bad things." "You can't earn lots of money honestly." "Money makes you arrogant; you forget where you came from." "To make lots of money, you have to neglect your family." "Once you have money, people will take advantage of you." "More money, more problems." What do we call people who have a lot of money? "The filthy rich." With all this, why would anyone want to make a lot of money?

Yet most of us have other, more positive beliefs about money because we've seen what money can do. Money can help us support our families. Money can make us more comfortable. Money can give us more choices. Money can pay for health care, travel, retirement. Money can be used to benefit others—our children, charities, our community. And *not* having money can be very painful. Most of us have such conflicting beliefs about money, is it any wonder that we find finances such a difficult subject?

Conflicting beliefs about anything prevent us from using the whole power of our minds and hearts to focus on what we want. If you want a relationship but are worried about losing your freedom, how likely are you to get into a great relationship? If you want to have kids yet also want a career, will you be happy with either choice until you resolve that conflict? If you want to make a lot of money but believe you'll have to give up spending time with your family to earn it, will you feel good about the sacrifice?

Even when people have actually begun to get ahead financially, their negative beliefs about money can make them unhappy. So many clients come to see me the first time and they're very nervous. They don't want anyone to know they're doing well because they think others will believe they're stuck up and arrogant. They're afraid they're going to be swindled, taken, or harassed by crooks or even poor relatives. "The more money you have, the more problems you have," they'll say. They're uncomfortable about the level of success they've achieved. It's almost as if we have an internal thermostat that allows us to make only so much money and still be comfortable—we have a comfort zone when it comes to our success.

Our comfort zone is usually based on a combination of beliefs that are based on what we've seen in our families and communities when it comes to money and what we think we deserve ourselves. If things start getting too hot—if we make a lot of money, especially all of a sudden—then we start doubting ourselves, feeling unworthy. We may even sabotage our success by overspending, acting like idiots, or simply worrying so much about money that we can't enjoy what we have. Eventually we drop back to whatever level of financial success we feel comfortable with.

I've seen the effects of this kind of "comfort zone" with clients who leave the barrio and move to primarily Anglo communities. First of all, their families tell them, "*Se te va subir a la cabeza,*" which means "You're going to get a big head" (see Barrier #6). They go through feelings of guilt for leaving the neighborhood and deserting their community. Maybe they look around the new neighborhood and start feeling out of place (another way of saying "out of their comfort zone"). It can get so bad that people react in one of two ways: they either cut themselves off from their community and their roots or they give up and move back, settling for less than they really want.

But here's the secret: *Our comfort zone and our thermostat are controlled by our beliefs—and what we believe about money is only true for us because we believe it, not because it's some universal truth.* "Money is the root of all evil"? If you look up what the Bible really says in the first Book of Timothy, chapter 4, verse 10, you'll find: "*El amor al dinero es raiz de toda clase de males.*" The *love* of money—not money itself—is the root of all evil. Money isn't good or bad; money is only what you make of it. You can earn it honestly or dishonestly. You can spend long hours away from your family making it, or you can invest it so your money works hard for you rather than the other way around. You can let other people cheat you of your money, or you can learn how to handle it yourself. Money is like words: money has no value in itself, but what we *do* with it creates the meaning it has in our lives.

What we believe about money, good and bad, controls how we earn it and use it. What we believe will determine whether we master our money or our money masters us. That's why the entire first section of this book is all about beliefs. I'm not saying that the beliefs you have are right or wrong; all I'm asking is that you take a look and see what your current beliefs are and what they have produced. Are you happy with what's going on in your financial life? Are there some places where you'd like more abundance but somehow never have been able to create it? Are there places where you know you have unresolved conflicts about money? When we decide to eliminate any old, lousy beliefs that have been holding us back and adopt positive beliefs around money instead, then we can make and use money responsibly, with enthusiasm.

To develop positive beliefs around money, we simply need to remember all the *good* things that money can bring—greater freedom, increased security, more choices, the ability to contribute to our families, our communities, and ourselves at a higher level, the chance to take advantage of the opportunities that life offers us along the way. And we need to realize that how we earn and use our money is a proving ground for our own strength of character. When we respect money as a valuable tool and as a means to attain the things we want in life rather than the thing we want for itself—when we understand that money simply magnifies our own inner strengths and weaknesses—then money is not the root of evil, but the basis for *financial greatness* for ourselves and our families.

Where You Are Is Determined
by What You Believe

Many wise men and women through the ages have told us that our lives reflect our thinking. Therefore, if today you are earning $60,000, it's because of the way you're thinking. If you're earning $250,000, it's because of your thoughts and beliefs. If your life is more focused on scarcity than abundance, you probably have scarce beliefs. To change the level of abundance you attract, you must first and foremost change the way you think and what you believe.

As a financial planner, I have clients who come in and say to me, "I'm working 40 hours a week and I make $30,000 a year. I know that for my kids to be able to go to college and for me to be able to buy a better house, I'll need to make $60,000 a year. But that would mean I'd have to work 80 hours a week. I'd never have time for anything else!" These clients believe that what they are earning is equal to the time and effort they're expending. But that's nothing but a belief, and, quite honestly, it's not necessarily a true equation. So I ask them, "How much do you think the CEO of your company is making? Is it more than $90,000 a year?" Usually they reply, "Of course. She makes hundreds of thousands of dollars." "So she's working over 120 hours a week in order to get paid that much? Or is she just getting paid based on the value she provides rather than the hours she works? Are there a lot of other people who work 40 hours or less and get paid more than $30,000? And if that's true, then perhaps in order to double your income you wouldn't need to work 80 hours. Perhaps there's a way to make more money simply by changing jobs, or getting promoted, or studying a new skill that would make your time and effort more valuable commodities." At that point many of my lower-income clients look at me in astonishment, because they've never thought that way before. Their beliefs had locked them into a certain vision of what they could have in this world. Once those beliefs are questioned, however, many of my clients step gladly into a world of greater possibility.

To live more abundantly, you need bigger goals, and to have bigger goals you must think differently. By doing so you might make the people around you uncomfortable, but you have to follow those thoughts with actions. In my own family I've seen the effects of changing beliefs about money. When my wife, Angie, and I got married, we decided to move to Irvine, California, a very nice area of Orange County that was close to my two children from my first marriage. When Angie told her best friend where we were moving, however, her friend gave her the "big head" routine. "Who do you think you are? Why are you moving to an Anglo community? You're going to be so far away." But we persisted because it was right for us. Shortly after we moved, Angie's friend started visiting us regularly. After a while she said, "Wow, this is a nice neighborhood, and the people are really friendly here." The next thing we knew, she was saying, "Maybe my husband and I should move to Irvine, too." When you are open to new, more positive beliefs, new possibilities of all kinds open up. And then your new beliefs can influence others to do, be, and have more, too.

If you're really committed to a life of financial greatness, your beliefs have to support you in your efforts to have a better income, build a better family, and so on. Financial greatness requires a high level of focus on achieving your goals. You can't

sabotage yourself—and therefore, you have to get rid of any conflicting beliefs you might have around abundance, scarcity,
money, and your own worthiness. Getting rid of beliefs is so simple, yet most of us believe it's difficult or impossible to do so. But
most of our beliefs are things that we make up, or we've heard
from other people. We have never tested them, and in fact, we
don't know whether they are true or not. "Money is the root of all
evil"? How do you know that, when money can do so many good
things in good people's hands? "To make twice as much, I'll have
to work twice as many hours"? Maybe, if you keep doing exactly
the same job at exactly the same wage. But aren't there a lot of
people who make more in the same number of hours? It's like
the story of the Christmas ham I told in the Introduction. Angie
and her mom thought that cutting the ends off the ham was what
made it taste so good, when in reality the grandmother had cut
the ends off to make the ham fit in the pan.

Three Simple Steps to
Changing Your Beliefs

The first thing to do is *look at the results you've been getting in your
life.* Are you making the kind of money you'd like? Are you experiencing the kind of abundance you and your family deserve? If
not, what beliefs are holding you back? Make a list of every negative belief you have around money, abundance, scarcity, deserv-
ing, and so on. You might be surprised at what you come up with.
Once you have your list, for each belief ask yourself, "How is this
belief working for me? Has it brought me what I want? What

results have I created with this belief?" If the results aren't what you want, then it's time to make a few changes.

The next stage starts by *looking at your old beliefs and asking, "How is this not true?"* Come up with examples from your own life that show these beliefs up for what they are: lies that are holding you back. If you can't come up with examples from your own life, come up with examples from other people's lives. Like the CEO I spoke of earlier—she doesn't have to work 120 hours a week to make triple what my client was making. There are plenty of people out there who do great things with money: establish foundations, help the disadvantaged, contribute to causes they believe in, and so on. There are many families who use money to become closer by going on vacations together. Nice guys can finish first. Find examples of ways your old, negative beliefs about money, abundance, and so on, aren't true.

Now comes the fun part! You get to choose what you want to believe. *For every old negative belief, come up with a positive belief to take its place.* Money is the root of all evil? No, money allows me to do good at a much higher level. I can't make any more money unless I work longer hours? No way—there are lots of ways to make more money that I can explore. I can upgrade my skills, get a better job, get promoted. Once you have your new beliefs, keep reading them over and ask yourself, "How is this true?" The more ways you can come up with that make you certain of the new belief, the easier it will be for you to incorporate it into your life.

The definition of insanity is doing the same thing over and over and expecting different results. Not changing your beliefs and expecting the same results is insanity. Conflicting beliefs hold you back from achieving what you want and deserve. It's like trying to drive a car by stepping on the gas and the brake at the same time. Get rid of your conflicting beliefs, and you'll find the road to financial greatness will be much smoother, and you'll reach your destination much more quickly. And you'll also enjoy the trip a whole lot more!

Part Two

Creating Financial Greatness:
The Journey Begins

I n Part 1 you saw some of the cultural beliefs that many Latinos have about money. These beliefs don't usually hit us in the face; instead, they sneak up on us, appearing whenever we're faced with a financial decision. I call these beliefs "potholes on the road to financial greatness" because they slow our progress, and sometimes stop us altogether.

But now that you know about these beliefs, I hope you will be able to see the potholes before you step in them and choose another path. Awareness is always the first step in changing a belief. Once you're aware of these cultural myths, you can say, "¡Ve te de aqui!"—"Get out of here!"—to the barriers that have held you back, and instead choose beliefs that will help you accelerate your journey to the financial security and abundance you deserve.

The second part of this book will show you how to develop your own personal road map for the journey to financial greatness. This map will be different from anyone else's, because your situation and goals are different from anyone else's. The main fault I find with most financial books (and, indeed, most financial plans and the planners who create them) is a lack of recognition of the uniqueness of each individual. Not just their financial situation—their assets, liabilities, resources, requirements, and so on—but what's more important, their *human* situation—their dreams, desires, relationships, goals, fears, and needs. Your road map won't work for you unless it maps out the specific road to the specific destination you want. And if you're not absolutely clear on what that destination is and what you're willing to do to get there, you stand about as much of a chance of reaching financial greatness as a traveler trying to cross the desert at high noon with no guide, no map, and no water.

Culturally, many Latinos have problems talking about their ultimate financial destination simply because they have trouble envisioning it. When I meet with my clients, I often say, "Imagine I had a magic wand that I could wave over your head and make things perfect. Tell me about your future. Where do you want to be? What's your lifestyle? Would you be at home or working? What would your children be like? What kind of home would you live in? Where would you shop? What activities would you enjoy? Describe everything that you'd want in your perfect life. Paint me a picture of where and how you'd want to be. Where do you see your marriage 10 years from now? Where do you see your kids when they're 18?"

You'd think such a wonderful daydream would be easy to visualize, wouldn't you? But far too many of my clients can't articulate their vision. Even more of them look at me with a blank stare because they can't imagine such a life. I think this happens for a couple of reasons. First, many Latinos don't think that far in the future because of Barrier #7: God takes care of the future so you just have to worry about today. Second, and far more serious, I don't know if these clients believe that they have the *power* to create the lives they desire. And without the belief in their own power to affect their destiny through their actions, there's no reason to visualize a future any brighter than their current circumstances.

I hope that by reading Part 1 you've realized the power of your beliefs in shaping your life and your future. I want to make sure you start reading Part 2 with one supreme belief in mind: *You are the only one responsible for creating your life.* Certainly, circumstances will play a part, but only a small part. I'm sure you know of people who started out with nothing and created businesses, raised amazing children, contributed to their community, and amassed enough wealth to retire comfortably and in great happiness. And I'm sure you know of others who perhaps had many advantages while they were young and wasted them all, ending up poor, alone, and unhappy. Circumstances never dictate the end of the road of our lives; they merely change the paths we take to get to our destination. Where we end up is determined by how we respond to our circumstances, not the circumstances themselves. And how we respond is directly affected by what we believe about ourselves, and what we desire. Even more, how we respond is affected by the vision we create for our lives.

The Power of "Why"

With all the great financial information that you can now obtain, why is it that most people continue to struggle financially? What is holding them back from financial greatness? After years of experience of working with financial planning clients, I have come to one conclusion as to why people have scarcity in their lives: They don't know *why* they are doing what they are doing. Mostly, they don't take the time to reflect on who they want to become and the kind of life they want. Knowing *what* to do with money is rarely the issue. With such an abundance of financial information about wealth—books, newspapers, magazines, TV and radio shows—why is it that most people end up broke? The reason most Latinos don't attain financial greatness is that (1) their beliefs (which we discussed in Part 1) keep them from pursuing financial greatness, and (2) they don't have enough compelling reasons—enough whys.

Let's take a look at the typical financial planning process with an average financial adviser. In the first planning meeting you are asked to gather and bring to the second session all your financial documents, including a budget, net worth statement, your most recent bank and investment statements, your insurance policies, and your most recent tax return. In the second meeting the financial adviser compares your current situation to your predetermined goals and makes product recommendations to help cover any gaps. In the third meeting you come in to reposition your assets and make some kind of investment or insurance purchase.

This is the typical financial planning process, but it works for fewer than 5 percent of the people who come in wanting a financial plan. For the other 95 percent, this process is weak at best. Why? *Because the goals that most people list are weak.* When people come to see me to plan their finances, most of the time they say things like, "I want to retire at 55," or "I want to save for my son's college education," or "I want to invest my money." But those goals are general and superficial. I call them "politically correct" because most of the time the people sitting in front of me are only repeating what they *think* they should have as goals.

How does the typical financial planner respond to these types of goals? By suggesting some type of investment or insurance product that will enable this person to save for retirement, or save for their son's education, or invest their money. But then life happens. (There are always plenty of life obstacles to distract us from our goals.) The client loses a job, or there's an unexpected medical expense, or the car breaks down and there's a big repair bill. What happens to those financial goals in those circumstances? They go out the window because they were weak to begin with. Weak financial planning goals are nothing more than New Year's resolutions, made quickly because you're supposed to make them at a certain point, and abandoned just as quickly when they become inconvenient.

It takes time to figure out what you really want from life. It takes longer than the couple of hours that a financial adviser schedules for you on his or her calendar. It takes your figuring out what's truly important to you and why, and then devising the goals, systems, and strategies that will help you achieve what you really want. But it's a sad fact that most people never work on their lives. The majority of humankind just goes on living day-to-day without the foggiest idea of the great lives they were meant to have. Unfortunately, at the end of our days we all wind up in the same place—and I don't mean financial greatness. Much as we try to avoid thinking about it, at the end of our 50, 60, 70, 80, or 90-plus years, ready or not, we have to leave this world behind. But what makes each of us unique are the different journeys we take to that designated "departure station." And that journey is completely under our own direction and power.

Recently I flew to Atlanta with my wife, Angie. As I boarded the plane and walked through the first-class cabin to get to my seat in coach, I remembered an earlier trip when I had flown first class and how much nicer the experience was. After Angie and I sat down, I said to her, "This flight is just like life. Everyone on this plane is going to arrive at the same destination. Sure, some passengers are going to get there with more comfort and more choices, but the final destination is the same. In life, everyone's final destination is death. We're all going to end up at the same place, but some of us are going to travel with more style, and comfort, and choices. Some of us are in first class, some in coach, and unfortunately some are in cargo. The question is, how do we want to make the journey?"

Luckily, there is a power inside us that can help us direct our journeys from this point forward. It's the power of our own whys, our own individual reasons for living, breathing, and existing. Discovering those whys is the first step of the financial planning process. Once you know why you want to succeed financially, and those reasons are exciting to you, then everything else falls into place. I'm not saying you don't have to make the effort: You have to do each of the 10 steps consistently in order to create consistent results. But when you have good, strong, personal reasons for taking action, then it's a lot easier to get yourself out of bed each morning and go out there to create the life of your dreams.

The power of why also helps prevent burnout—the "Is that all there is?" syndrome. In my office, I have a number of clients who have achieved quite a bit of success financially. They come in to see me, and often they confess they no longer enjoy what they're doing. Twenty years ago they started a business or got into a profession or became a doctor because they loved it. But now they've worked so long and so hard that they hate the idea of going to their job one more day. Then there are the people who, in my opinion, are even sadder. They've worked at a business for 20-plus years while they neglected the other parts of their lives. Now their health is suffering and their spouses are divorcing them. Their kids are completely alienated because their workaholic parent barely knows who they are. These poor people are looking around at their successful business lives and saying, "Is this all there is?" They've sacrificed everything to be successful, only to realize that by most measures they're not successful at all.

With these clients, the first step in the financial planning process is to help them get their life priorities clear, to figure out why they wanted to start a business or be a doctor in the first place. We also explore what's truly important to them—family, community, success, money, health—and in what order those things need to be to create a truly fulfilling life. Then, and only then, do we start setting goals and devising strategies to help them achieve what they truly want. These goals may have nothing to do with money but everything to do with spending more time with their kids, or providing a happy home for their aging parents, or contributing time to a charity or social cause that's dear to their hearts.

When my clients finally see the big picture of how they can be fulfilled in many different areas of their lives, I watch relief spread across their faces. Finally, they start to believe that it's possible to live a life filled with happiness instead of stress, health instead of overwork, abundance instead of scarcity, relationships that are rich in love and connection instead of alienation and accusation. They leave my office excited and committed to putting their plan into action. And over the months I get the pleasure of watching my clients make their dreams come true.

Financial greatness may seem to be only one element of a fulfilled life. But by my lights, the only way to be financially great is to be great in every other area of your life as well. That's why creating financial greatness is an idea that goes beyond the typical financial planning process you read or hear about. The journey on the path to financial greatness is simple—but it does take time. I assure you, though, it will be time well invested. In fact, the best investment you can make in your financial future right now is time. On Page 92 we talked a little about the power of compounding, how a small amount of money invested for a long period of time increases geometrically. In just the same way, the time you invest now in planning your financial future will compound to help you create a financially great life.

The key to creating financial greatness is one word: focus. The 10 steps to financial greatness are designed to help you focus with laserlike precision on exactly what you want to be, do, and have in your life. The process will show you how to balance the different areas of life—health, wealth, relationships, recreation, spirituality, community, and so on. You'll learn to accomplish your dreams while avoiding the trap of burnout. Most important, you'll learn how to enjoy the journey, evaluating your progress and celebrating every win as you keep moving toward your ultimate goal of financial greatness.

The 10 Steps to Financial Greatness

Over the years I have used my 10-step process to create financial greatness for many of my clients. It is a truly rewarding experience, and I am excited to make this process available to you.

Each of the next 10 sections describes a step in the process. Don't worry—you don't need a financial degree to understand anything! All you really need is a willingness to learn, a little honesty, and a commitment to completing all 10 steps. But this process has to be done actively. Don't just read the section and say, "Wow! That was interesting—but the ball game is on TV, and the kids are calling. I'll get back to working on the steps later." When you sit down to read a chapter, grab some paper (a journal would be better) and a pen or pencil and do the step. Decide to get through all 10 steps in a specific period of time—two weeks, a month, 90 days, whatever is doable while still creating a little pressure on you to keep going.

I've done my best to make this process simple, fun, and rewarding. I'll use lots of examples to show you how the process is done. Most important, I promise you that when you arrive at the end of your journey, you will experience the most overwhelming, incredible, fulfilling feeling. Time and time again I have seen my clients overcome with tears of joy when they see for themselves what is possible when they realize that financial greatness is in their grasp.

In truth, the journey to financial greatness is more like a wheel than a straight line. That's because the priorities and needs of our lives change over time. We have one priority when we are just starting a business, for example, and another when the business is running well. We need to spend a lot more time focused on our kids when they're young, and our relationships with them will change once they leave the nest. The 10-step process allows us to renew and reevaluate our priorities when appropriate.

Chart 1, a circular model, is a visual representation of the process. Basically, all you will be doing is answering 10 questions. The next 10 chapters will explain each of the steps in turn. There are also exercises that will help you put these steps into action for yourself. At the end of each chapter you'll see a clear list of questions and actions that will make each step very easy to accomplish. Mark the chart's location so you can return to it whenever you need to remember the overall design of the 10 steps to financial greatness. This is your road map. Follow it, and you'll be amazed at how quickly you achieve results you only dreamed of before—or perhaps never even had the courage to envision.

Are you ready to begin? Let's start the journey!

Chart 1: 10 Steps to Financial Greatness

Step 1: What Are Your Major Life Focus Areas and Roles?

Step 2: What Are Your Core Values?

Step 3: What Are Your Ideal Outcomes and Goals?

Step 4: What's Your Starting Point?

Step 5: What Obstacles May Get in Your Way?

Step 6: What Are Your Available Resources?

Step 7: What's Your Strategy?

Step 8: What Practical Systems Must You Set in Place?

Step 9: Monitor Your Progress Along the Way

Step 10: Celebrate and Share Your Success!

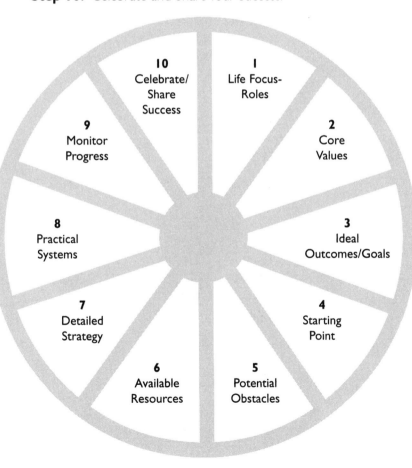

Step #1

What Are Your Major Life Focus Areas and Roles?

t has been my experience that most of us get caught up in the daily grind of everyday life. And often it's not until a tragic event happens that we get some perspective on how fragile life really is. Most people work so much *in* their lives that they forget to work *on* their lives. We forget to see what is truly important. For most, life is just a blur. Day after day, we constantly put out fires. We're always running, never taking time to reflect. We're always focused on the urgent, never the important.

Let's take a look at a typical day for a working wife. She gets up an hour earlier than the rest of the family. She showers, dresses, and puts on her makeup. She wakes her kids and tells them to start getting ready for school. She goes to the kitchen and starts preparing lunches for the kids while at the same time struggling to make breakfast. The kids need to get their hair brushed or a paper signed for school, and all of a sudden she's running late. She puts the kids in the minivan, drops them off at school, and then drives to work in bumper-to-bumper traffic. Nine hours later she is back on the road, driving to pick up the kids either from school or day care. It's now 6:30 P.M. and she needs to start making dinner. "Oh, what the heck," she thinks, "It's too late to start cooking, I had a rough day at work, and at this point I sure don't want to have to wash any dishes." So it's out to get burgers, or she orders a pizza and buffalo wings and a 2-liter bottle of soda. By 7:30 P.M. the kids are finished eating dinner and almost done with homework; it's time for her to make sure some laundry gets done and the kids take a bath. She watches a little television while ironing the kids' clothes. It takes about an hour (on a good day) to put all the kids to sleep. She ends the evening picking up around the house. Exhausted, she collapses into bed and falls asleep.

This is the typical day for the typical Latina. (Where was her husband? His day wasn't as hectic, but almost.) And guess what? Tomorrow is another day just like it, over and over and over again. Mounting debt, children getting bigger, and both parents getting older. This is not a journey to financial greatness. This is the journey to despair and frustration, a journey of constant struggle. How do we get out of this pattern? How do we stop living lives of quiet desperation and break free to the lives we truly want?

As I said earlier, the journey to the life of our dreams begins by figuring out what those dreams are and then creating a plan of how to get there. That's what you will be doing in the 10-step process. While at first it may seem like we are taking the long way to financial greatness, every part of this journey is necessary. Think of it as devising the perfect route for you to get from where you are to where you want to go. It's kind of like going to the American Automobile Association and getting one of their specialized maps called TripTiks. When you go to AAA, you tell them, "I want to go from Los Angeles to New York City," and they will give you a little booklet of maps customized just for you. Each map shows a 50-mile section of the best route for you to take between Los Angeles and New York City, with the road you should take marked in red. That's exactly what you will have when you finish the financial greatness process: a road map specific to you, showing you exactly where you need to go and what you need to do to achieve what you truly want.

But in order to figure out your unique road map, you need to know the big picture first. After all, there are a lot of roads that will take you from L.A. to New York. You need to decide what route will suit you best before AAA can plan a trip for you. You can tell them, "I want to take the northern route," or "I'd like to stop through San Antonio to see my cousin Lupe." In the same way, once you're clear on the different areas of your life that are important—your big picture—then you can create a financial plan that will help you get wherever you want to go.

I call this big picture your *major life focus areas* or functions. They are the parts of your life that need some level of attention at one time or another. When all of these areas of life are in alignment, you have balance and peace of mind. When they're out of alignment, you end up like the Latina in the earlier example, constantly busy but with no sense of fulfillment at the end of days, weeks, months, or years.

Defining Your Major Life Focus Areas

The first step to planning your journey to financial greatness is to step back and look at your life from a different perspective. It's like getting an aerial view of what's really important to you. Later, you're going to get more specific about each of these areas.

Answer these two questions:

1. What are the most important major areas of my life?
2. What areas would I have to work on to feel truly successful?

Like a living, breathing organism, our life has functions that must be tended to. We must breathe. We must drink water. We must eat. We must move. If we don't carry out these functions, we will wither and die. In the same way, if you don't take care and nurture certain major functions in your life, your whole life becomes unbalanced and unfulfilled.

Chart 2 shows some typical life focus areas to get your thinking started. This is the diagram I created for my own life. I've included a blank diagram at the back of book (page 239) if you wish to use this format for your life focus areas. Or, if you choose, you can simply list the areas on a sheet of paper or in a journal.

Through my years of doing this process with my clients, I have noticed that most people have roughly nine life focus areas. My list includes the following:

Chart 2: Major Life Focus Areas and Roles

Physical

Intellectual

Spiritual

Relational

Professional

Personal growth

Material

Charitable

Financial

All of these areas are in my life daily and need some level of attention if I want to have what I would consider a great life. Your list may be somewhat different, but I believe that many of these areas should be part of your focus if you wish to take the journey to financial greatness.

The life areas you choose to focus on are great indicators of your priorities at any given moment. Once you've put your own list together, the second step is to take a look at it with a critical eye. Ask yourself, "Are there areas missing that could cause me problems later on?" Lots of people pour all their attention and focus into a couple of areas, like career or family, and completely forget that there are other parts of life that need to be priorities as well. I tell my clients, "Okay, let's talk about some of these life focus areas: for example, health. Even if you have a lot of money 30 years from now, if you don't take care of your health today, what kind of shape will you be in to enjoy it? Diabetes is the number one killer among Latinos. Many of us have very poor eating and exercising habits. If you're not going to care for your health, money is not going to help you. I'd strongly suggest you make health one of your areas of focus."

The second question is "Are there areas I am overfocusing on right now that are throwing my life out of balance?" So many people are very successful in business but end up getting a divorce because they don't make relationships a focus. "But getting my business off the ground has to come first!" they protest. Perhaps—but how do you think their spouses feel knowing they are second, third, fourth, even last in the list of priorities, if they're on the list at all?

If you're focusing only on work and not focusing on relationships, you may end up with a lot of money but no one to share it with. In the same way, if you're putting all your attention on work and career and no attention on managing the money you earn and saving for the future, you could definitely experience pain. And if your whole focus is on yourself, your work, and your family, and you're not paying attention to what I call your responsibility as a human being—on charitable/spiritual/community areas—then you're missing out on some of the most satisfying and fulfilling parts of life. Your wheel of life focus areas need to be balanced. If they're not, it's like trying to drive a car with a tire that's flat on one side. Your journey to financial greatness is going to take a lot longer and there will be a lot more bumps along the way.

Determining your major focus areas is a great way to look at your life from a broader perspective, and to see all the crucial elements that make up a great life. The idea is to work *on* your life, not just *in* your life. Decide what area or areas you want to focus on, knowing that eventually you will have to put some focus on all areas to attain greatness.

Defining Your Roles

Within each life focus area, we often assume a number of different roles. In our career, we may be an employee, a marketer, an entrepreneur. In our relationships, we are a friend, a spouse, a parent, a child, and so on. In the area of contribution, we may be a volunteer, a contributor, or an organizer. The roles we play help us define who we are and what's important to us. They are how the different life focus areas appear on a day-to-day basis in our lives.

Take a moment to look at your list or diagram of your life focus areas. Ask yourself, "Within this life focus area, who am I? What roles do I play?" Under each life focus area, write down the roles that are most significant and important to you.

When I do this process with my clients, I tell them, "Imagine you're waking up on a typical morning. What's the first role you have to play?" For many of my clients, it's either "spouse" or "parent." "Great," I say. "What's the next role?" This may be "boss" or "employee" or "businessperson" or "caregiver"—whatever their particular occupation. We go through an entire typical week and identify the roles they play on an ongoing basis. Then we return to the life focus diagram, and I ask, "Now, for those life focus areas you haven't been making a priority but want to from now on, what roles would you like to fill in those areas? In the area of health, for example, would you like to be an athlete? A strong, toned, sexy lady? A fit exerciser? In the area of finance, do you see yourself as an investor? A creator of wealth? A saver?" We make sure that every life focus area has at least one role attached to it. Roles take the big areas of life focus and help make them more specific.

However, we not only need to know what roles we play but also how important those roles are to us in creating a fulfilling life. So take a look at your own list, and for each role ask yourself, "On a scale of 1 to 10, how important is this role? And am I fulfilling that role at the level of importance I've given it?" Many of us might rate the importance of being a great husband or wife at a 10, but admit truthfully that we're only acting like it's a 4. So ask the next question: "What will it take for me to achieve this rating for this role?"

Again, when I work with my clients, the dialogue often goes like this. "Rosa," I ask. "You say one of your roles is a wife. How important is that role to you?"

"It's a 10," she replies.

"Great—and on a scale of 1 to 10, what kind of wife are you?"

"Well, I can't spend a lot of time with my husband since I'm working, and the kids take most of our focus . . . probably a 6."

"Okay," I say. "What do you think would make you a 10 as a wife? Tell me everything a level 10 wife should be or do." Once we've gotten Rosa's list, I tell her, "This is just a starting point, Rosa. Do you think that knowing what your husband would consider a level 10 wife would be important?"

Rosa looks at me, puzzled. "I never thought of that. But sure, I want him to think of me as a level 10 wife."

"So I want you to go home and ask him what he thinks a level 10 wife should be and do," I suggest. "And then make one more list for yourself. We learn most of what we do as husbands and wives from the way we saw our parents treat each other—both what to do and what not to do. So think of your own mother and the way she was in her relationship. Was she a level 10 wife? If not, what would have made her great? With those three lists—yours, your husband's, and the list about your own mother—you should be able to come up with a pretty good picture of what you need to do to be a level 10 wife."

Knowing what your roles are, how important they are in your life, and how you can fulfill those roles at the level you wish, are all part of getting the big picture of your life, both how it is now and how you would like it to be from now on. This stage is absolutely critical in beginning the journey to financial greatness. If you say to me, "Louis, I want to come to your office. Can you give me directions?" I have to know where you're coming from, because depending on whether you're starting out in Long Beach or downtown L.A., the directions will be very different.

This discovery of roles can also reveal the same kind of imbalances that you found when you looked at your life focus areas. In the area of career, for example, you may be so completely focused on being a great boss, producing results and meeting quotas, that you neglect your role as coworker. If this happens, are you really being a great boss? Probably not. Among Latinos, family is an extremely important life focus area. Many Latinos will list being a parent as one of the most important roles they fill. But they will end up neglecting a role that also has an enormous impact on family: the role of spouse. Husbands and wives never get to know each other. They don't work on the marriage, and as a result divorce rates in Latino communities are just as high as in any other community in the United States.

The last part of this step is to choose the roles and areas you need to focus on, based on what will create the greatest impact in your life at the present moment. This does not mean that you neglect the other roles—that's part of the reason your life may be out of balance now. Think of it like going to the gym. If you want to get into great shape, you have to do different exercises for different parts of your body. You will need to do cardiovascular exercise for the heart. You can do sit-ups or crunches to get your abs into shape. You may lift weights to build up your arms and chest, and perhaps do squats or use a stair-climbing machine to firm up your legs. But depending on what kind of shape you're in, some areas may need more work than others. So you do a few more crunches, or lift heavier weights for a while until that muscle group is stronger and closer to the fitness level of the rest of your body. But that doesn't mean you stop doing your cardiovascular exercise! Every area needs a certain level of continuing attention and focus in order for the body to be healthy.

In the same way, for a while you may need to put more focus on a particular area or role so you can build up your strength there. If you've neglected your marriage, you may need to take better care of your spouse. If you've ignored your health, you'd better make it a priority. If you're a better boss than coworker, maybe it's time to build up your work relationships. If your focus has been exclusively on business and you haven't taken care of your own spiritual needs or given anything back to your community, then you may need to expand your vision and look both inside and outside for greater fulfillment. Remember, your goal is to have a balanced "wheel of life," where there are enough life focus areas to make your days feel rich. Each area needs to receive enough attention to keep it running smoothly along the journey to financial greatness.

The Story of John

Let me give you an example of the power of knowing your life focus areas and roles. A couple of years ago, John came into my office wanting to do some education planning for his three boys, ages 14, 12, and 9. He was making excellent money but had very little to show for it, even though he was working 6 days a week. I told him that before we did any type of education planning I wanted to know what was truly important in his life. I took him through the questions in this chapter and discovered John's life focus areas: career, finances, relationships, spiritual, and physical health.

Then we looked at the roles John was filling in each area. When it came to relationships, "father" was the very first role John listed. It was clear John loved his boys very much, and his role as a father was very important to him. In fact, on a scale of 1 to 10, 1 being not important and 10 being most important, his boys were an 11.

I asked John, "If I were to meet your three boys when they were grown up and asked them the question, 'What kind of father was John to you?' what would you like for them to say?"

"I hope they say I was a great father," John replied.

"If I were to ask your boys what made you a great father, how do you think they would respond?" Before he could answer, I added, "John, it has been my experience that for most kids the word 'love' is spelled T-I-M-E. Most children don't care how big a home they lived in, what kind of car their parents drove, or how many toys they had when they were growing up. What we value from our childhood are memories. Some of us are fortunate to have great loving memories about our parents, and some of us are not. John, what kind of father did you have?"

John smiled. "My father was great."

"What made him great?"

"I was an only child," John told me. "My father was a sailor and loved the sea. I vividly remember that when I was 15 my father took me on a four-week sailing trip, just him and me. To this day I can still smell the ocean air and taste the salt water, and I can still see my father's strong hands. My father taught me how to be a man on that trip. We talked for hours about what it meant to be a man. That was the best memory I have of my father. He passed away when I was 18 years old, and because he didn't have any life insurance my mom had to sell our sailboat to bury him." I could see the tears in John's eyes.

"That's a great story," I said. "Have you shared a great moment like that with your three boys yet?"

"No, I haven't," he replied.

"If you could create a wonderful memory with your three boys, what would you do?"

John thought for a second and said, "I would love to teach my children the love of the sea. I would love to take them on a sailing trip."

"What's stopping you, John?" I asked.

"I'm too busy at work, and I have very little savings," he said sadly. "A sailing trip like that would take time and money. But if I could do that, I could die tomorrow and be happy."

Right then and there we called John's boss. I introduced myself as John's financial planner and explained to his boss that I was doing some financial planning for one of John's greatest life goals. To achieve his dream John would need to take some time off, about three weeks, the following year. I asked the boss if that would be all right. John's boss explained that the company was already experiencing a shortage of qualified employees and that it would be tough to guarantee it. I explained what we were doing and shared John's story—and John's boss gave him the okay.

Once we knew John's life focus area and the importance of his role as a father, and we had come up with the goal of the sailing trip, I had John go back and create a budget (his strategy). We then set up a system: we established an account so that every month a portion of his paycheck would go toward the trip with his boys. Within 14 months, John's dream of sailing with his three boys had become a reality. And John's life and his sons' lives will never be the same.

When John came to my office that first day, he thought that he wanted to do some education planning for his boys. Instead, he got an education on how to build a great life. He left my office excited about his plan and committed to following it through. John is now saving consistently for his sons' future college tuition costs, but he now also saves money to make memories with them as well.

Knowing your life focus areas and roles will allow you to experience greater fulfillment, not just at the end of the journey but on a daily basis. In the next step you're going to discover how your values—the emotions and things you consider most important in life—can help point you in the direction where your own path to financial greatness lies.

EXERCISE

Step 1: What Are Your Major Life Focus Areas and Roles?

Ask yourself the following questions. Write the answers on a sheet of paper or in your journal, or make a copy of the diagram on page 239 and write your answers there.

Determining Your Life Focus Areas

▶ *What are the most important major areas of my life?*
    Suggestions include physical, intellectual, spiritual, relationships, professional/career, personal growth, material, charitable, financial, etc.

▶ *What areas would I have to work on to feel truly successful?*
Are there areas you have been neglecting that you need to focus on now in order to create a more fulfilled life?

▶ *Are there areas missing that could cause me problems later on?*
Have you forgotten about your emotional and spiritual needs? Are you saving for the future? Are you giving back to your community?

▶ *Are there areas I am overfocusing on right now that are throwing my life out of balance?*
Are you putting too much energy and effort into work? Are you pouring all your time and focus into your relationships and neglecting your health?

    Now that you've learned your current life focus areas and discovered which ones need to be added, emphasized, or deemphasized to create a more fulfilling life, you're ready to determine your roles.
    Within each life focus area, ask yourself the following questions. Write your answers under the appropriate life focus area, either on the chart, on a sheet of paper, or in your journal.

Determining Your Roles

▶ *Within this life focus area, who am I? What roles do I play?*
List all the different roles you have in each area. For example, under relationships you might have friend, child, parent, spouse. You may also find you have only one role in a particular life focus area, and that's fine.

▶ *On a scale of 1 to 10, how important is this role? And am I fulfilling that role at the level of importance I've given it?*
Take each role and give it a rating on its importance. Then be very honest and evaluate whether or not the way you're filling that role is meeting your own standards.

▶ *What will it take for me to achieve this rating for this role?*
If you discovered a gap between how you want to fill this role and how you're filling it currently, brainstorm ways you could do better. Find role models, people who have filled this particular role well, and ask, "What about them made them a great (parent, spouse, boss, athlete, etc.)?" If you want to be better at a role that involves others (like a parent or a spouse), ask the people who would be directly affected how they would like to see you act in that role.

Congratulations! You now have the big picture of what to focus on in your life in order to attain fulfillment. This is part of creating the power of why that we spoke about earlier. You're ready for the next step: discovering the values and emotions that you want to feel daily and that will propel you along the path as you journey to financial greatness.

Step #2

What Are Your Core Values?

Why do we do what we do? Why do we work, get into relationships, go to sporting events, give back to the community? Because our actions make us feel certain emotions that we consider pleasurable and important—that is, valuable. We call these emotions *values*. To travel to financial greatness, we need to know what is important to us in life—not just the things, but the feelings, the relationships, and so on. Your values are the compass that will keep you on track to living a great life. Your core values define who you are. They also direct your actions. Without a focus on your values you will be distracted by events that eventually will have very little meaning. Once you know the values that are important to you, it's a lot easier to create a list of goals that will help you feel good on a regular basis.

We value different feelings in the different areas and roles of our lives. And while we probably don't spend a lot of time think-

ing about them, defining our values in any context is actually
very simple. We just ask:

"What's most important to me? What feelings do I want to
have in this particular area/role/context?"

Assuming you've created your own list or diagram showing
your life focus areas and roles (if you haven't done it yet, go back
to Step #1 and do it *now*), you can write these values next to or
underneath each of the different areas and roles. If you have an
area of "profession" or "career," for example, you may have a
value of respect, or "accomplishment," or "progress," or "success." Those are all feelings you want to experience in the area of
career on a regular basis. A sample is shown in Chart 3.

In the area of relationships, you may list the roles that are
important to you—spouse, parent, friend, family member, and so
on—but you also should list the feelings that are important to
you in each of those roles. For example, in my life focus area of
relationships I have named being a husband as one of my important roles. One of the feelings I want as a husband is intimacy. In
my role as father, I value love. In my role as a friend, I value caring and fun. And so on.

Everything we do in life, we do so we can get a particular kind
of feeling. Do we go to work so we can bring home a bunch of
paper called money? Not really. We go to work so we can feel successful, or secure because we know we are taking care of ourselves and our families, or have a sense of connection with the
people we work with. Similarly, what do we want from any relationship? Feelings. The feelings are what motivate us, not the
work or the relationship or the money. Those feelings will drive

Chart 3: Major Life Values

our actions, and our choices about life and money. Can you see why knowing your values could have such an enormous effect on your journey to financial greatness?

More important, the feelings that you want may be very different from the feelings someone else wants. Take a look at the area of finances, for example. In Chart 3, you can see that I want to experience a feeling of freedom when it comes to finances. Many of my clients, however, tell me they want a feeling of security. Do you think my clients and I would make very different choices when it came to managing our money because we want different feelings? You'd better believe it.

Indeed, values even determine whether we *realize* when and if we've achieved financial greatness. Take a look at Juan and Maria. Juan's most important value regarding money is safety. His father lost everything in a bad business deal when Juan was a child, so Juan wants to make sure that such a thing can never happen to him or his family. The reason he wants money is to feel safe, and he works 80-hour weeks to put aside enough money to take care of any possible disaster. When I asked Juan how much money it would take for him to feel safe, he replied, "At least $2 million: $1 million in government bonds, and a business worth $1 million with no debt." Juan figures it's going to take him another 20 years to put away $1 million in bonds and build his business. In the meantime, he worries constantly whether he's making safe decisions for his business and his family.

Maria, on the other hand, has a value of choice when it comes to finances. The reason to have money, she feels, is that it gives her the ability to do what she wants when she wants it in the way she would like to do it. When I asked Maria how much money it would take for her to feel she had choices, she answered, "An income of $100,000 per year from investments." She figures that with the money she's put away (some in bonds, some in mutual funds, some in real estate), and with the way her business is growing, she can reach her goal within about 10 years. Because Maria values choice in her financial area, she's very open to trying different strategies both in her business and personal finances. She has had some failures and successes, but she's learned from her failures and is able to make better choices the next time. When I asked Maria where she would consider herself on the journey to financial greatness, she told me, "You know, I may not be at greatness yet, but I definitely feel I'm on the road. I already have so much choice in my life financially, and I'm confident that the choices I'm making overall are very good."

Both these people are making progress along the road to financial greatness, but Maria is enjoying a lot more fulfillment than Juan simply because of the difference in their values. Notice the other important point: it's not just the value but *how you define that value* that makes a difference. Which leads to the second question. Once you've defined a feeling (value) you want to have in a life focus area or role, ask:

"What does this feeling mean to me? How do I know that I have achieved this value?"

You should be able to come up with a sentence or two that describes exactly what each value means to you. If you wrote down "love" as a value, how will you know you have love? Do you have to be in a committed relationship? Do you need to have a bunch of kids? Do you need a large circle of friends? Do you need to live near your brothers, sisters, parents, or cousins?

For example, as a husband I value intimacy. I know that I have intimacy in my marriage when I feel my wife is the most important person in the world to me and she feels the same way about me. In my friendships I value caring, and I know I have caring when I feel my friends are there for me and I'm there for them. Remember, these statements don't have to be long and involved;

just write down a few words about what this particular value means to you.

By the way, if you're in a committed relationship, either romantic or professional, it can be enlightening to share your values with your partner and vice versa. How many marriages have gone bad simply because the partners valued different things, or even had the same value—love—but had different ways of feeling and showing it? Similarly, in a professional relationship it's vital to know what's important to your business partner.

Again, this step may not seem directly related to the journey to financial greatness, but I hope you see how vital it is. Knowing what feelings are important to you, and how you know when you have those feelings, allows you to plot a road to financial greatness that will provide you fulfillment along the way and not just at the end. It also allows you to have a far more abundant and exciting life in every area—finances, relationships, profession, and so on. You'll know both the targets you're aiming for and how to shoot so you'll hit them far more often. And that will mean a lot more bull's-eyes and a much happier life.

What Are Your Core Values?

Look at each life focus area and the role(s) in it, and answer the following questions. Write the answers on a sheet of paper or in your journal, preferably on the diagram or page where you have already listed your life focus areas and roles.

▶ *In this particular life focus area or role, what's most important to me? What feelings do I want to have in this particular area?*
For career or professional, for example, you may want success, accomplishment, respect, security, and so on. For relationships, you may list love, fun, affection, closeness, caring, etc.

▶ *For each value or feeling I have listed, what does this feeling or value mean to me? How would I know that I have achieved this value?*
Each of your answers should be no more than a sentence or two. For health, for example, you may have something like, "When I feel fit," or "When I feel my body is toned, trim, and working like a machine," or "When I eat, drink, sleep, and exercise in a healthy way," and so on.

Remember, this list of feelings will help you not only reach your destination on the journey to financial greatness, but it will also help you to enjoy the journey a lot more. Now that you understand a lot more about your life in general, you're ready to create a plan for the journey. You can now move into creating a clear list of outcomes and goals that will help you achieve fulfillment in all your life focus areas and roles.

Let's keep moving!

Step #3

What Are Your Ideal Outcomes and Goals?

After identifying your major life focus roles and values, you're ready to set some powerful and compelling goals that will motivate you to overcome any obstacle in your journey to financial greatness. This is the step where most people start. They decide, "I want to save for my kid's education," or "I want to retire at age 55," or "I want to move to a bigger house next year." Those are all very important goals. However, they aren't linked to the *whys* that will truly motivate these individuals: their vision, life focus areas, roles, and values. When you link a goal to an area, role, and value that are important to you, then you're a lot more likely to follow through when the going gets tough.

Knowing your life focus areas, roles, and values will also help you set goals that will get you what you truly want, not what you think you *should* want. Remember the story of John on page 127?

He thought what he wanted was to do some education planning for his sons. But what he really wanted was to provide exceptional experiences that his sons would remember all their lives. The goal that excited him was to buy a sailboat so he could share his love of the sea with his children. I was able to help him set up his finances so he could do both: buy a sailboat to take his children sailing and also save money for their college education.

The goal you think you want may not actually get you the feelings and results you truly desire. All of us have only a certain amount of money at our disposal, so we want to leverage our money based on what matters most, based on our life focus areas and roles. To show you what I mean, let me share with you some typical discussions I have with clients.

Scenario 1

PABLO: Hi, Louis, my wife and I are here because we want to start saving for our son's college education.

LOUIS: How old is your son?

PABLO: He's 16. I know that we should have started earlier, but we just haven't had the money. You are the third planner we've seen and we are so confused. One planner recommended we put money in a Section 529 plan. Another planner recommended that we use an education savings account. What do you suggest?

LOUIS: What I suggest is that we don't look at any investments or savings programs at this time. Let's take a look at what is truly important for your son. Let me ask you a few questions. What is your son's grade point average?

PABLO: He's a C student.

LOUIS: On a scale from 1 to 10, 1 being lowest and 10 being highest, where would you say your son would be in regard to his self-esteem?

PABLO: Maybe a 5.

LOUIS: By now, he probably has taken the PSAT test. Where did he score?

PABLO: He didn't do all that great.

LOUIS: You see, Pablo, as important as it is to have savings for college, it is more important that your son succeed in the critical areas that determine college success. If your son has poor grades, poor self-esteem, and poor placement exam tests, even if you saved $1 million in the next two years, you still couldn't guarantee that your son would get into a great college and succeed.

PABLO: I guess you're right.

LOUIS: So, what is it you truly want for your son?

PABLO: We want to see him happy, educated, and successful. We want him to be able to take care of himself without our help one day—you know, that day when we're not here.

LOUIS: Well, since you tell me he's doing okay but not that great in school right now, how about taking some of the money you were planning to set aside for college and using it to hire your son a tutor, get him involved in some self-esteem workshops or seminars, and enroll him in an SAT prep course? I'm sure it will be money well spent and will dramatically increase the chances of your son getting into and graduating from college.

Do you see how important it is to know what you truly want before you start setting goals? This family will help their son a lot more by investing in his education today with prep courses and tutors, than by putting aside money for a college education that the boy might not even use unless he gets help right now.

Let's look at a different scenario: retirement planning.

Scenario 2

SARA: Hi, Louis. We are here because my husband and I decided we need to start saving for our retirement. We have been so busy with our lives over the last several years. With both of us constantly working and raising our children, we had no idea how fast the time would fly. We are now in our late forties and haven't even started to save for retirement. We need your help.

LOUIS: Great. First, I'd like to ask you a few questions. Tell me what is important to you in your lives.

SARA: Our children are everything to us. We have lived for them. But we think that now it's time to start thinking about us.

LOUIS: Wonderful. So, tell me about you, about your marriage. On a scale of 1 to 10, 1 being least important and 10 being most important, how important is your marriage to you?

SARA: Obviously, it's a 10.

LOUIS: Now, on that same 1-to-10 scale, where would you rate your marriage right now? Is it a 10? Tell me the truth.

SARA: Well, maybe a 5.

LOUIS: Where on that scale would you have to be to contemplate going through a divorce?

SARA: A 2.

LOUIS: You're at 5 now, and 2 would mean divorce. . . . That's not a lot of distance, is it? You know, couples never want to think about divorce, yet almost 6 out of 10 people these days go through it. My fear is that if you start setting assets aside for the future before you focus on your current situation, all that we might be doing is saving the money for a divorce attorney and not your future.

SARA: I never thought of it that way. I don't want us to end up divorced.

LOUIS: What would have to happen to get your marriage back up to a 9 or 10?

SARA: We need to reconnect. The children have been such a focus that I think we really don't know each other anymore. We need to spend more time together. We need to learn how to communicate better.

LOUIS: Fantastic. We'll work on your retirement, but first let's focus on how we can use some of the assets you plan to use toward retirement and shift them to making your marriage a 9 or a 10.

In the case of this particular couple, they allocated a certain amount each month and spent it on enriching their marriage. They took courses together, they went away on weekend trips by themselves, they even took dancing lessons so they could have a hobby they could enjoy together without the kids. Their marriage is a lot stronger because they're not only planning for a great future together but they're also enjoying the present.

The last example is one that few of us consider when it comes to financial planning, yet it can be the most important when it comes to even having a future to plan for: taking care of your health.

Scenario 3

MIGUEL: Hi, Louis. Thank you for seeing us.

LOUIS: My pleasure. How may I help you?

MIGUEL: My wife and I are here because we had a major scare recently. I had a heart attack and realized that if I had died, my wife wouldn't have been prepared financially. We don't have any savings, little insurance, and no estate plan. My business is dependent upon me, and it would be difficult for my wife to take over, especially since our two kids are still in grade school. We want to start saving for our future.

LOUIS: What did the doctor say about your heart attack?

MIGUEL: He told me that my business has created undue stress. I haven't been able to exercise since I started my business three years ago because of time constraints. I have also gained 30 pounds in those last three years.

LOUIS: Tell me, on a scale of 1 to 10, 1 being not important and 10 being most important, how important is your health?

MIGUEL: Are you kidding me? It's an 11. I just haven't had the time. But now I know that I must make the time.

LOUIS: So on that scale of 1 to 10, where has health been up to this point?

MIGUEL: Probably a 2. It's just that there always seems to be an emergency at the office that is more important.

LOUIS: Do you agree with me that if you don't take of your health you might not *have* a future? Do you agree that no amount of savings could replace you for your family? Do you agree that you've got to make some changes, even if they're tough?

MIGUEL: I guess I don't have a choice.

LOUIS: Miguel, I'll help you establish a financial plan that will provide your family with the security you want. But why don't we focus some assets right now to help you get healthy? Some suggestions would be to hire a personal trainer to get you back in shape, and perhaps a nutritionist to change your eating habits. If your health is an 11 on a scale of 10, then you need to make it a priority and take action right now. Wouldn't you agree?

MIGUEL: You're right. Thanks.

LOUIS: You're welcome. I will make sure that we place a line on your budget for a personal trainer.

To create great life goals, you must identify the ideal outcomes that will satisfy your most important life functions, roles, and values. For example, as a professional who has a value of success, what outcomes or goals do you need to achieve in order to feel successful in your profession? (That's a very different question than asking, "What do I have to accomplish in my job?") In your role as a husband in the area of relationships, what outcomes or goals will help you achieve a value of intimacy? Or as a parent, what outcomes will help you communicate love (a value) to your children?

You may find you end up with several outcomes for the different life focus areas, roles, and values in your life. That's very normal. We may have many different goals in our job, for instance, or different outcomes in the area of health. If you have more than one outcome in any area, you need to prioritize them: put them in order, with the most important outcome first. Life being what it is, it's very easy for goals and outcomes to fall by the wayside. But there are some goals that are absolutely vital for our progress on the journey to financial greatness. Those are the goals you list first.

Clarity and specificity are the keys when it comes to creating your goals. Clarity has tremendous power to engage both yourself and others in helping you achieve your dreams. The clearer and more specific you are about what you want, the easier it will be to attain. Ask yourself questions like, "What will this goal look like when I have attained it?" "By when must I accomplish this goal?" "Is this goal realistic?" (If you're 5 feet 2 inches and have a dream of becoming an NBA basketball player, we need to talk.)

Then you need to get emotional about this goal. Our minds and will can take us only so far when it comes to putting in the work required to accomplish anything. For that extra burst of motivation, nothing beats attaching a lot of emotion to accomplishing your dreams. Ask yourself, "How great will it feel when I have this goal in my life?" "How bad will I feel if I don't accomplish this?" "Who will I become once I have this goal in my life?" When you engage the power of your emotions with the strength of your mind and will, you'll be unstoppable. Your goals will seem to be easily within your grasp.

The final questions concern the importance of this goal in your life. Is this goal a "must," just a "should," or merely an "It would be nice"? Ask yourself, "On a scale of 1 to 10, how important is this goal to me?" Now, you may find that the goal receives less than a 10 rating based on your past experience. As in the scenarios I described earlier, was the second couple's marriage a priority of 10? How about Miguel's health in the third scenario? But what priority did those goals *need to be* for my clients to experience fulfillment in their lives? Level 10 or higher. So, after you know what priority this goal is or has been, ask yourself, "What priority does this goal *need to be* for me to experience fulfillment?" You can follow up with the question, "If I were to accomplish it, what level of impact will this goal have on my life?"

If your answers to the last two questions are 10, then this goal is a must for you. And, based on experience, I believe that unless your answer to both questions is "10," you most likely won't attain that particular goal. However, the only way to figure out whether a goal is a 10 is to be clear about the goal and how it fits within your life focus areas, roles, and values.

For goal setting to be anything other than daydreaming, you have to put time, energy, and thought into creating goals with meaning. And that means you have to think about your life. But as my dad always told me, thinking is hard work—that's why so few people do it. When you put in the thought, however, when you know what your life focus areas, roles, and values are, when you create goals based on those areas, and you can answer "10" to the last two questions, I guarantee you will have enough ammunition to get through most obstacles. You will have what I call financially great goals!

Goals at this level create a burning desire to get accomplished. They burn with an internal flame that is not put out by any unexpected rain. The goals that are 10s come from within, from your own needs, desires, and dreams. If you don't take the time to go within, you will go without.

Step 3: What Are Your Ideal Outcomes and Goals?

For each role in each life focus area, answer the following questions. Write the answers on a sheet of paper or in your journal. Make sure you list the goals for each life focus area and role, and that the goals are tied to the values you associate with each. For example, if you have a life focus area of finances with a role of investor, and your value is freedom, what goal can you devise that would allow you to be an investor who is moving toward a feeling of freedom?

Determining Your Ideal Outcomes and Goals

▶ *What goals must I have in this area/role in order for me to feel (value)?*
In the area of health and the role of athlete, the question might be, "In my health (life focus area), what goals must I have as an athlete (role) in order for me to feel fit (the value)?" Make sure your goals are very clear and achievable. "Get closer to my wife" is not clear; "take my wife away on a second honeymoon" is a lot more achievable.

▶ *What specifically do I mean by this outcome/goal?*
Write in complete detail, with as much clarity and vision as you can, what your goal will look like when it is attained. After you have written down your goal, ask yourself how you could make it more specific.

▶ *What's my deadline for accomplishing this?*
It's often said that a goal without a deadline is just a dream. Set a realistic time frame for accomplishing this particular goal.

▶ *Is this goal realistic and within my control?*
If you're 5 feet 2 inches you could be a great athlete, but you probably won't become the center for the Los Angeles Lakers. Make sure that your goal is

realistic for you and within your control. You can't plan on winning millions in the lottery, but you can plan on putting aside money so you can have millions when you retire (as long as you start young enough).

▶ *What will it feel like to attain this goal? How great will it be?*
Write down all the emotions you would feel. Would you jump up for joy or yell at the top of your lungs? Would you treat yourself to something special? The more emotion you attach to getting this goal, the more likely you are to achieve it.

▶ *How will it feel if I don't attain my goal? How painful will it be?*
Would you feel regret? Unhappiness? Terrible sadness? If it wouldn't feel that bad, maybe it's not such an important goal. Get yourself into the state of actually feeling as bad as you would if you missed out on this particular goal.

▶ *When I reach this goal, who will I become? What kind of person will I be when I reach this important goal?*
Will you be smarter, happier, kinder, gentler, more successful, more loving? I know many individuals who reached financial success yet never attained financial greatness because they became the opposite of what I just listed. Remember to pack as much emotion as you can into your answers. Make sure they include the feelings you listed under your values for this role.

After you have written your goals, you need to choose the ones you want to start working on. Your next step is to put your goals in order of importance. Ask yourself the following questions, and based on your answers, rewrite your list of goals in order, the most important goal first.

Prioritizing Your Goals

▶ *On a scale of 1 to 10, how important is this goal to me?*
Be honest. The worst thing you can do at this point in the process is try to look good to yourself.

▶ *On a scale of 1 to 10, how important does this goal* need to be *for me to experience fulfillment and greatness in my life?*

Take a look at your life focus areas, roles, and values. They should give you a very clear idea of the importance this goal needs to have.

▶ *If I were to work on this goal, on a scale of 1 to 10, how important would attaining this goal be in my life?*

If your answer here is anything but a 10, you have two choices. First, you can move the goal lower on your list. Second, you can write down all the reasons this goal would affect your life in positive ways. When we know something is "good for us," sometimes we resist telling ourselves why. Yet those emotions and reasons are what will keep us pursuing our goals when the going gets tough. Now is the time to get excited about your goals, so you will keep traveling the road to financial greatness.

Congratulations! You now have a clear list of powerful goals and outcomes for all the different areas of your life. You have put those goals in order of priority, and I hope you're excited about starting to work on them. But before you do, you need to be equally clear about the point you're starting from. That's our very next step. Read on!

Step #4

What's Your Starting Point?

Now that you truly know what you want, why you want it, and what purpose it's serving, you need to know where you are starting. Has anyone ever asked you for directions to your home or office? Don't you need to know where they are coming from to give them the best possible route? In essence you're asking where their starting point is. It's no different in your journey to financial greatness. If you want directions on how to get there, you need to know where you start. You need to write down where you are now in comparison to where you want to be. The difference between your starting point and your final destination—financial greatness—is the "gap" that the journey is designed to cross.

Determining your starting point is something financial planners (like me) should help you do. In order to create a solid plan, we need to know what your current assets and liabilities are, what your current income is, whether you own your own home or business, how many children you have, and so on. All of these figures help determine your financial starting point. However, as you should have realized by now, the journey to financial greatness isn't just about finances; it's about living a great life in every single area and role that's important to you.

That's why this step begins with your own honest assessment of where your life is right now. For each of your life focus areas and roles, you need to ask, "On a scale of 1 to 10, where am I in this particular area or role?" Remember the clients I talked about on page 140? Pablo's son was at about a 5 in his self-esteem. Sara's marriage was about a 5. Miguel's health was so important to him that he rated it as 11, yet he realized that up until now it had been a 2. All these numbers gave my clients an idea of where they were starting from on their journey to financial greatness.

And yes, as part of determining your starting point, you will need to get a clear picture of where you are financially. You'll need to know your assets and liabilities, your monthly expenses, net worth, investments, insurance policies, and so on. The form at the end of this chapter can help you put together those numbers for yourself, or you can consult a financial planner.

Now, you may be saying, "But I'm no good with numbers, Louis!" You don't have to be. But you do have to be smart enough to consult someone who is, because this step is absolutely critical. There's an old Chinese proverb that says, "A journey of a thousand miles begins with a single step." I always add, "And getting that first step off on the right foot will determine how well and how quickly that journey will go."

Knowing your starting point and your destination is not only important but also necessary. How can you get to a destination if you don't know where you're going? But equally important, how can you get there if you don't know where you are starting from? No one can give you directions or guide you without knowing your starting point. And if you set out without a clear idea of where you're coming from, you might get to your goal by chance or luck but the odds of your getting there are very slim. On the other hand, when you know exactly where you're starting from and where you want to go, you can plan your route between those two points with relative ease. Sure, there may be a lot of different roads you can take, but at least you have an idea of how to get from point A (your starting point) to point B (financial greatness)!

Step 4: What's Your Starting Point?

For each role in each life focus area, answer the following questions. Write the answers on a sheet of paper or in your journal, preferably next to the appropriate life focus area and role.

Determining Your Starting Point

▶ *On a scale of 1 to 10, where am I in this particular area or role?*
Remember, this is not where you want to be but where you actually are right now. Be honest, but at the same time, don't dump on yourself if you're not where you want to be. This question is to help you simply discover where your journey to financial greatness is starting. If you wanted to travel to New York City, for instance, you wouldn't judge yourself based on whether your journey was starting from Los Angeles or San Antonio or Miami or Chicago, would you? But it would still be important to know what city you were coming from so you could travel in the right direction.

▶ *What assets do I possess in this particular area/role?*
Part of determining your starting point is realizing the strengths you have that will help you in the journey. For each life focus area and role, list your strengths. Do you already have a great relationship with your children? Does your spouse regard you as a good provider, or a great companion? Are you great at communication at work or at sales? Are you a good detail person or an excellent planner? Write down any traits, relationships, gifts, or advantages that you already possess and would consider helpful in your journey. (We will discuss this more in Step 6.)

▶ *What liabilities must I deal with?*
Do you have any traits or problems that might get in your way? In the area of health, for example, do you have any physical limitations that might prevent you from exercising regularly? At work, have you had problems with

your boss or coworkers in the past that might affect your future efforts? (We will discuss this more in Step 5.) Again, don't use this as an excuse to beat yourself up. Be honest but realistic. There are no obstacles you cannot overcome with enough time, effort, and will.

Determining Your Financial Starting Point

In the area of finances, determining your starting point is both easier and more complicated. Easier because it all comes down to numbers that are very easily measured. (Where you're starting from in a marriage, for example, is often a lot harder to put a number to. What you may consider a 5, your spouse may think of as a 2 or a 7.) More complicated because many people think of numbers as complicated and difficult. In reality, however, these numbers will be based on things you should be able to figure out without a lot of effort.

Your financial starting point comes down to four numbers: (1) your assets; (2) your liabilities; (3) your income; and (4) your monthly expenses.

Assets

This number includes everything you own that has a cash value, either now or in the future. I'm going to list several different types of assets. If you own that particular type of asset, write down what it is and how much it's worth. This will include your home (if you own it) and car (ditto). Put the current value of each asset, even if you don't plan on selling it. (You probably wouldn't sell your home unless you were moving somewhere else, for example; but for most of us, our home is one of our biggest financial assets.) Also, do not deduct any mortgage or car loan amount from the value of your home or car. Those numbers go under "liabilities."

You may also have a life insurance policy for yourself or your spouse. Some policies (mostly whole-life policies) have a cash value. With cash value life insurance, you pay a monthly premium. That money pays for the insurance and any administrative costs charged by the insurance company, and the remainder can be invested by the insurance company in either fixed or equity investments, depending on the type of policy. As the owner of the policy, you can cancel the policy, pull out the money you've invested (the premiums you've paid minus insurance and administrative costs) and use it in emergencies. Many people take out an insurance policy during their income-producing years and then use the policy's cash value to supplement their income once they retire. You may be charged fees depending on when and how you cancel a policy and take your cash, but the cash value of a life insurance policy should be considered an asset.

CURRENT ASSETS

Assets	Amount/Value ($)
Cash	
Savings accounts	
Money market accounts	
Money market funds	
Certificates of deposit	
Mutual funds (equity or bond)	
Individual stocks	
Bonds	
Other securities	
Notes receivable (2nd trust deeds)	
Stock options	
Tax-deferred annuities (Non-qualified)	
Individual retirement accounts (IRAs)	
Roth IRAs	
Pension plans:	
401(k)	
403(b)/TSAs	
457 Plan	
SEP	
SIMPLE	
Profit sharing (vested)	
Other pension	
Life insurance cash value	
Limited partnerships	
Personal residence	
2nd residence (vacation home)	
Investment property:	

Assets	Amount/Value ($)
Property 1	
Property 2	
Property 3	
Automobile	
Automobile	
Boat/RV	
Business	
Jewelry	
Precious metals	
Antiques	
Collections	
Other valuable personal property	
Other	
Total assets	

Liabilities?

Liabilities are any debts you currently owe. This would include mortgages on your home or other real estate (how much you have left to pay on them); car loans (same); credit card debt; other loans, either personal or business (include student loans if you are paying them off now); and so on. This category is different from your monthly expenses, which you'll list in the last chart.

CURRENT LIABILITIES

Liabilities	Amount ($)	Interest Rate (%)
Mortgages on your home (current amount left to pay)		
Mortgages on other real estate		
Car loans (amount left to pay)		
Business loans		
Credit card debt		
Student loans		
Other personal loans		
Total Liabilities		

Monthly Income?

To determine your starting point, you need to know how much income you bring in each month. For most of us, this is simple; we get a monthly or weekly paycheck and can calculate our income based on that. However, if you have income from sources other than work, you need to include this income in your monthly total.

List what you bring in before taxes—income, property, etc. Taxes will be listed under monthly expenses.

CURRENT MONTHLY INCOME (BEFORE TAXES)

Source of Income	Amount per Month ($)
Your income from employment or business (before taxes)	
Spouse's income from employment or business (before taxes)	
Income from rental property	
Income from pensions	
Income from Social Security or other government stipends	
Income from dividends, trusts, annuities, insurance policies, etc.	
Other (any income not included in the above list)	
Total income per month	

Monthly Expenses

How much you spend each month on living expenses is a big factor in determining your starting point on the journey to financial greatness. If you're spending more than you're making, obviously you're not going to go very far very fast! Getting a clear picture of where your money goes is one of the most important steps in starting your journey. Many of us don't realize how much money we're spending each month, so we're puzzled when we can't make more progress financially. On the other hand, you may have a very clear idea of how much you spend and just want to know how you can cover those expenses and still have money left over for the future.

If you're not sure how much you spend in any of these categories, track your expenses for one month. You'll probably be surprised how much you spend in some categories.

MONTHLY EXPENSES

Expense Category	Monthly Amount
Home	$
Rent/mortgage	$
Mortgage (2nd or equity)	$
Other loans on residence	$
Association dues	$
Home (renter's) insurance	$
Property taxes	$
Maintenance	$
Gardener	$
Housekeeper	$
Household products	$
Home furniture/fixtures	$
Home/holiday decorations	$
Total Home Expenses	$ Total
Utilities	$
Electricity	$
Water	$
Gas	$
Waste (trash)	$
Telephone	$
2nd phone line (Internet)	$
Cell phone/pager	$
Total Utilities Expenses	$ Total
Auto	$
Auto loan/lease payment	$
Auto insurance	$
Auto registration fees	$
Gasoline	$

(chart continued on next page)

Expense Category	Monthly Amount
Auto maintenance/repairs	$
Parking	$
Public transportation	$
Total Auto Expenses	$ Total
Children	$
Child support	$
Child care/babysitting	$
Child clothing	$
School support/events	$
School tuition	$
Extracurricular/tutoring	$
College funding	$
Total Children Expenses	$ Total
Food	$
Groceries	$
Breakfast out	$
Lunches out	$
Dinners out	$
Coffees/smoothies/etc.	$
Total Food Expenses	$ Total
Clothing	$
Work clothes	$
Casual clothes/misc.	$
Shoes/accessories	$
Dry cleaning	$
Total Clothing Expenses	$ Total
Travel	$
Vacations	$
Day/weekend trips	$
Total Travel Expenses	$ Total
Entertainment	$
Cable TV/movies/rentals	$
Concerts/ball games	$
Books/mags./newspapers	$
Music/CDs	$
Hobbies	$
Total Entertainment Expenses	$ Total

Expense Category	Monthly Amount
Personal	$
Life insurance	$
Disability insurance	$
Continuing education	$
Technology	$
Postage	$
Bank service charges/fees	$
Gym dues/sports gear	$
Personal care (hair/nails/etc.)	$
Entertaining/parties	$
Total Personal Expenses	$ Total
Medical	$
Medical insurance	$
Dental insurance	$
Long-term care insurance	$
Doctor/dentist/optometrist	$
Chiropractic/therapist/etc.	$
Glasses/contacts	$
Prescriptions	$
Insurance deductibles	$
Total Medical Expenses	$ Total
Gifts	$
Birthdays	$
Christmas	$
Anniversary/special events	$
Total Gifts Expenses	$ Total
Pets	$
Pet food	$
Veterinarian	$
Pet miscellaneous	$
Total Pet Expenses	$ Total
Savings	$
Retirement qualified	$
Retirement nonqualified	$
Current savings/investments	$
Total Savings Expenses	$ Total

(chart continued on next page)

Expense Category	Monthly Amount
Charitable	$
Church	$
Nonprofit organizations	$
Other	$
Total Charitable Expenses	$ Total
Personal Loans	$
Credit card: Visa	$
Credit card: MasterCard	$
Credit card: Amex	$
Credit card: Dept. Stores	$
Credit card: Other	$
School loans	$
Other loans	$
Total Personal Loans Expenses	$ Total
Professional Fees	$
Accountant	$
Attorney	$
Financial adviser	$
Other consultants	$
Total Professional Fees Expenses	$ Total
Taxes	$
Federal	$
State	$
SDI	$
FICA	$
Medicare	$
Total Taxes Expenses	$ Total
Miscellaneous	$
Alimony	$
Walking-around money	$
Unreimbursed employee expense	$
Union dues/fees	$
Miscellaneous	$
Negative on rental properties	$
Total expenses:	$

Tips:
1. When an expense is annual, divide by 12 and enter.
2. If you don't know the amount, make an educated guess.
3. Review your check register for expenses.

You now have a picture of your own personal starting point—not only financially, but also where you're starting in every important life focus area and role. You're now ready to chart your course to financial greatness. But have you ever driven down a freeway during rush hour and listened to the traffic reports on the radio? The traffic reports tell you when there's an accident or construction or any kind of delay on the road, so you can either (1) allow extra time to get where you're going, or (2) take a different route to your destination. In the same way, in the journey to financial greatness you will probably encounter certain obstacles. It's very valuable to know what those obstacles might be so you can plan your trip accordingly. Turn the page and get ready to take your next step!

Step #5

What Obstacles May Get in Your Way?

ave you ever noticed that when things are going along smoothly, inevitably some obstacle pops up? Your career is moving forward and all of a sudden a new "hot shot" gets the promotion you thought was yours. Your family life is great, and then you discover another baby is on the way, and you have to stretch your budget to cover the additional expenses. You thought the money in your IRA was safe, only to discover you had too much money in tech stocks and the value of your portfolio has dropped by 40 percent in a year. Your exercise program is on track, but one day at the gym you feel a "pop"— you've pulled a muscle in your back and can't exercise for a month while you recover.

Such obstacles are the potholes, roadblocks, detours, bad weather, and other unforeseen emergencies that you will eventually encounter on your journey to financial greatness. Notice I said that you *will* encounter. Life inevitably gives us obstacles. I guess they were put there for a purpose. Maybe life doesn't want things to go too smoothly for too long, just in case we were to get lazy or flabby. Perhaps obstacles are life's distractions: they crop up to tempt us to take our eyes away from our goals. Perhaps obstacles are a way of life asking us, "How badly do you want what you're going after? Are you willing to put in the effort even when the going is tough?"

Obstacles come in many different forms. There are internal and external obstacles, obstacles created by circumstances and obstacles created by our own beliefs and emotions. I've encountered an enormous range of obstacles, both in my own life and in discussions I've had with my clients. Since it's important for you to identify your own obstacles, and since you may not have considered some of these things as obstacles in the past, I'm going to list different challenges I've seen in my clients and give you a short description of how these obstacles may show up in your life. As you read them, ask yourself, "Have I ever felt this way? Is this what's held me back? How has this particular obstacle affected me?"

Here are some of the obstacles I have come across over the years.

▶ **Fear**

This is the big one. Fear holds almost everyone back at one point or another. We're afraid to start our own business. We're afraid to ask that special person out. We're afraid to make a commitment of our time, money, or resources. Fear can be a good thing when it causes us to look before we leap. However, for most of us it stops us from looking at all, much less leaping. Fear is like the toll gate on the road to financial greatness. We have to be willing to pay the toll, to (as a popular author once said) "feel the fear and do it anyway." Getting past our fears is the only way we'll get anywhere on the journey to our goals.

▶ Complacency

We all get stuck in our comfort zone—doing just well enough to get by and not seeking to do better because we're comfortable. But complacency is one of the greatest dangers we can face on the road to financial greatness. It's like a big, sticky swamp that holds us back from achieving what we're truly capable of.

What's most frustrating is that complacency is what we run into when we've achieved a little bit of success. We look around and compare ourselves to those who aren't doing so well and feel pretty good. When that happens, we're dooming ourselves to a life of mediocrity instead of greatness. To achieve our goals and make the most of our time on Earth, we have to fight our tendency to be complacent.

▶ Limiting Beliefs

Often the reason we're fearful is our limiting beliefs—about ourselves and our abilities, about what's possible, even about what we deserve. Every single one of the barriers I described in the first part of this book can get in our way on the path to financial greatness. Whenever I see clients who just can't seem to make progress in certain areas of their lives, I always ask them, "What's the barrier that's holding you back?" Inevitably there's something there.

Even when your circumstances aren't the best, it's always your response to the circumstances that's will make the biggest difference. And how you respond is based completely on your beliefs.

► Lack of Clarity

If you don't know what you want, how are you ever going to get it? If you don't know where you're going, how are you going to know when you arrive? That's why the first part of the financial planning process focuses completely on creating clarity: about the areas and roles of your life that are important to you, and the goals you want to achieve in each area or role. Fuzzy goals equal fuzzy results. The entire 10-step process is designed to make sure you are absolutely clear on what you want, why you want it, how you plan to achieve it, and how you will know when you've arrived.

► Lack of Time

This is the lament of the modern world. Is there a human being in the industrial world that hasn't said at some point, "I don't have the time"? But somehow we always make time for the things that are important. We eat; we sleep; we take care of our kids and families. For most of us, "lack of time" is just a convenient excuse. Usually it's not lack of time but lack of priorities or lack of motivation.

Remember at the beginning of this section when I talked about knowing *why* you're doing something? If you have a strong enough reason and a lot of emotion attached to a particular goal, then I guarantee you'll make the time to make it happen. If ever you find yourself saying, "I don't have the time," go back to that particular goal or area and review why it's important to you. Then make a commitment to devote at least 5 minutes a day to your goal. Even 5 minutes a day can make a major difference, and often 5 minutes a day can become 10, then 20, then however much time it will take for you to turn your goal into a reality.

► **Lack of Money**

This is the one that crops up with my clients all the time. They just don't see how they can squeeze any more out of their take-home pay to put into retirement savings, or to put toward their children's education, or to buy a piece of real estate, or even to put aside for a vacation. But how many of us could, if we wanted to, put aside $1 a day without really noticing that it was gone? How many of us could do that with $5 a day? Certainly, some people are struggling to make ends meet. But if it's important, somehow we manage to find the cash, don't we?

Because many of our financial goals are (1) very large, and (2) in the distant future, they are either overwhelming or not compelling, so we're less likely to deny ourselves small, immediate pleasures to save for our distant, long-term goals. But what's more important, buying a Starbucks coffee or saving for your retirement? Renting a video or DVD for an evening's entertainment or putting that money toward your child's college fund? It all comes down to motivation and priorities. Keeping those distant goals right in front of you, and staying connected to how great it will feel when you see your son get his college diploma or when you enjoy a comfortable retirement, will help you postpone the small pleasures of the present for much larger pleasures in the future.

► **Negative Emotions such as Jealousy and Envy**

We don't like to admit it, but negative emotions are some of the biggest obstacles we can face in the pursuit of our goals. Jealousy and envy are two of the worst, and they are products of one of the most unproductive traits of humankind: our tendency to compare ourselves with other people. Far too many of us look at those who have succeeded and say, "Why them and not me? Why do they think they're so hot?" Instead of recognizing successful people as guides whom we can emulate in our own journey to financial greatness, we turn them into roadblocks or distractions.

These negative emotions are closely associated with the beliefs about scarcity I talked about on page 70. We feel jealous and envious mainly because we think there's only so much to go around, and if that person has more, then we will end up with less. But nothing could be farther from the truth. You can choose to emulate successful people, or you can let your negative emotions about their success block your progress, but you'd better realize that the only one being hurt by your jealousy and envy is you. A better choice might be to look at successful people as trailblazers who have cleared the road for *you* to reach your goals more quickly. Thank them and get back on the road!

▶ **Health-Related Issues**

If you don't take care of your health, it can definitely prevent you from making progress toward your goals. But don't let ill health become an excuse for not taking some action. There are so many inspiring role models of people who have suffered horrible health challenges and still accomplished amazing things. Do you know the story of Art Berg? At the age of 21, five weeks before his wedding, Art broke his neck in a car accident. He became a quadriplegic. But he decided that being sick was not what he wanted his life to be about.

Art worked hard to become a renowned author, speaker, lecturer, and teacher. He was a world-class wheelchair athlete who set a world record in 1993 as the first quadriplegic to complete the ultramarathon between Salt Lake City and St. George, Utah—325 miles in 7 grueling days. Art also married his childhood sweetheart and they have three beautiful children.

As Art frequently remarked in his speeches, "The difficult takes time. The impossible just takes a little longer." The next time you think that there is any health condition that will keep you from achieving your goals, remember Art Berg and keep moving in the direction of your dreams.

► **Lack of Confidence or Self-Esteem**

Certainly, when we first begin something new there's always a tendency to find our confidence a little shaky. I always recommend that my clients take small steps at first, and look for every single way in which they've succeeded. You made out a budget? Great! You saved $25 this week? Fantastic! You went to the gym regularly for a week? Hooray! Small successes are what give us the confidence to keep going on the road to financial greatness; recognizing and celebrating them are what will build our self-confidence "muscle."

But a deeper issue—lack of self-esteem—can keep us from ever taking the first step into something new. Again, small victories can make all the difference in boosting self-esteem. I tell clients, "Look, God doesn't make trash, and God made you. If every human being was made in the image and likeness of God, who are we to feel unworthy?" Then I ask, "What's one thing you have done that made a difference in someone else's life? Who loves you? Would that person love trash? And if you haven't lived up to your potential so far, what can you do that would make this world a better place, either for yourself or someone else?" All of us are here for a reason. We may not know what it is, but I believe we're here to contribute in some way to the world. In some ways, we contribute simply by being alive. If you are alive, then you are accomplishing a purpose. And if you add to that purpose the goal of being the best you can be and contributing the most you can give, then your life cannot help but be great.

► Unsupportive Spouse, Family, or Friends

None of us exist in a vacuum. We all are part of relationships of some kind, and we have people who feel connected with us. Unfortunately, sometimes those people seem to want to hold us back just when we want to leap forward. It's a human trait to be uneasy about change, and those we love can be very nervous when they see us thinking, speaking, or acting in unfamiliar ways—even when those ways are more positive and happier! One of the core drives of humanity is a need for certainty, and change usually brings with it uncertainty. A husband wants to quit his job and start his own business. A wife wants to quit work to be home with the kids full time. A child declares he or she wants to apply to Ivy League schools for college. A friend starts a 5-day-a-week exercise program and no longer wants to meet after work for a few beers. All these changes may *be* good, but they may not *feel* good for the people around you. Your friends and family want the status quo back; they want what they're familiar with.

If your friends or family seem less than supportive of some of the goals you wish to pursue, realize that they may be afraid of losing you on some level. The best thing you can do is to reassure them that they are still important in your life. Make sure you connect with them, even if you feel you must change the way you do so. If you want to start your own business, show your spouse how you plan to continue to provide for your family, and how much better your lives will be when the business is up and running. If you don't want to go with your friends for those after-work beers anymore, find a different way to spend time with them. In most relationships, the form matters less than the feeling. As long as your friends and family feel you still love and care for them, and they recognize how important this new change is to you, then usually they will be willing to let you pursue your dreams.

► Lack of Self-Discipline

Self-discipline is usually produced by two things. First and most important is motivation. If you're motivated, you'll be disciplined. That's why the first three steps of this process are designed to give you the kind of mental and emotional motivation that will make you want to make consistent efforts toward accomplishing your goals.

The second factor that produces self-discipline is a system. Discipline is nothing more than doing what you need to do when you need to do it, and the easiest way to become disciplined is to create a system. Step 8 is all about creating systems that will make self-discipline much easier.

► Lack of Commitment

Again, this is usually a matter either of motivation or perhaps some internal conflict about the goal. If you have a goal of doubling your yearly income, yet you believe you won't be able to spend time with your family as a result—and family is one of your most important life focus areas—then your commitment to your financial goal may falter. One of the most valuable questions I teach my clients to ask is, "How can I (get my first goal) *and* (get my second goal)?" For instance, "How can I double my income *and* spend time with my family?" This kind of question starts them thinking in different ways, and helps them come up with alternative strategies they perhaps had never considered. Maybe the family could be involved in the business. Maybe a different business opportunity could help you earn more money in less time. Perhaps what your family wants isn't quantity but quality time, so instead of spending every night at home with you parked in front of the TV while the kids do homework, you make two nights a week "family nights" and do things together, and work on your business on the other weeknights.

Most of our goals are not mutually exclusive; it's just a matter of figuring out as many different ways as we can to get them. There are millions of paths along the road to financial greatness, but all of them ultimately end up in the same location.

► **Lack of Knowledge or Education**

To my mind, this obstacle is always temporary because we can always learn whatever we need to know to accomplish our goals. It's just a question of finding out what we need to know and how we can learn it, and then put in the effort necessary to do so. There are very few goals that require some kind of degree, certificate, or diploma, but even if they do—if your goal is to be a doctor, for instance, or a plumber, or a teacher—all you have to do is to make getting the education your first goal.

There are so many ways to acquire knowledge in today's

world. You can read books (like this one!); you can join a group of people who have the information you seek; you can find someone to teach or mentor you; you can get on the Internet and look up what you need to know. No one should let lack of knowledge or education get in the way of his or her dreams. Knowledge is like a golden coin: it will always possess great value. Pursue the knowledge you need as your first step in pursuing your goal.

► Lack of Experience

In my opinion, this is the lamest obstacle of them all. We *all* start with a lack of experience! None of us were born knowing how to walk or talk. But we kept working at it until we were toddling everywhere and talking up a storm. Whenever we start something, by definition we're not going to have any experience at it. The "lack of experience" obstacle is really nothing but fear of failure in another disguise. We're afraid of looking stupid or failing at this new endeavor, so we simply don't bother to try.

Do me a favor: commit to being really lousy at something the first time you try it. Make "lousy" your standard. Plan to be really bad for the first few times and make it okay to stink. Trying something and being lousy at it is a lot better than not trying at all. And trying something and being lousy at it is the only way you're going to get better. If you had stopped trying to walk after the first time you fell on your bottom when you were a baby, you wouldn't be walking today. I suggest you approach each of your goals as if you were a baby. The key isn't to look good or be good at it; the key to success is to keep trying. The only way you'll get the experience you're looking for is if you keep at it, again and again, even if your results are less than great. Eventually, you'll know exactly what to do and you *will* be great. You'll also be surprised at how quickly that will happen.

To get where we want to go, to achieve our goals and travel the road to financial greatness, it's essential that we identify the obstacles we are facing so we can figure out a way around, over, or through whatever is standing in our way. I can tell you from personal experience, it does no good to ignore obstacles, especially the internal ones, because they won't go away. Trying to make progress while ignoring your obstacles is like trying to run a marathon while ignoring the fact that your leg is broken. You're not going to make a lot of progress, you might cause permanent damage to yourself, and it's definitely going to be a lot more painful.

The key with obstacles is to prepare as much as you can in advance for them. You need to sit down and write down everything you can think of that you might eventually have to face so that you can prepare for it. Obviously, you can't prepare for everything, but you need to at least prepare for the obstacles that you know will come your way. Remember, the journey to financial greatness is supposed to be a fun adventure. Sure, there will be trials and tribulations at certain points. But if you can anticipate the obstacles and avoid most of them, you will reach your destination in much better shape than someone who just took off on the journey with complete ignorance of all the potential pitfalls.

A great general once said, "Know your enemy." That's what this step is all about—knowing the enemies you will face so you can vanquish them with ease. It's kind of like the video games that kids play. After a few games, the kids can tell you which monsters are going to appear in what settings. They also know exactly what they have to do to vanquish the monsters and move forward in the game. This step helps you identify your own personal monsters so you, too, can vanquish them and make progress on the road to your goals and dreams.

Step 5: What Obstacles May Get in Your Way?

For each goal, answer the following questions. Write the answers on a sheet of paper or in your journal, preferably next to the appropriate goal.

▶ *What are the external obstacles that I may face in pursuing this goal in this life focus area or role?*
These obstacles may include lack of time, lack of money, lack of support from friends or family, lack of education, knowledge, or experience, health challenges, and so on. List everything external that might possibly get in the way of your achieving this goal.

▶ *What are the internal obstacles that I may face in pursuing this goal in this life focus area or role?*
These would include any beliefs or emotions that hold you back from pursuing your goals with your full heart, mind, and soul. Lack of confidence or self-esteem, lack of self-discipline, fear, limiting beliefs, lack of clarity, negative emotions, lack of commitment all fall into this category. List every single emotion or belief that could prevent you from pursuing your goals wholeheartedly and enthusiastically.

Now, knowing the obstacles isn't enough; you have to prepare to overcome them. Answer the following question for each obstacle.

▶ *How can I prepare in advance to deal with this obstacle if and when it arises?*
For external obstacles, this may involve setting up conditions that will make it possible for you to pursue your goals no matter what. If your obstacle is lack of time, how can you organize your life so you have a certain amount of time on a regular basis to pursue this goal? If it's lack of money, how can you set aside a small amount of money every day that you can put toward your goal? If it's lack of knowledge or education, how will you get the information you need? You want to create a specific plan composed of easily

accomplished steps that will enable you to make steady progress toward your goals.

For internal obstacles, two things will help. First, reconnect with your reasons for wanting this goal. A wise man once said, "If you have a strong enough *why*, you'll always figure out *how*." Second, internal obstacles are usually some kind of belief about yourself, what you're capable of, or what you deserve. Ask yourself, "How is this belief wrong?" List at least a dozen reasons why you are worthy, why you should have confidence, why it's okay to be afraid when you start something new, and so on. Read your list of reasons again and again. And then take one small action every day that proves your internal obstacle is nothing but a figment of your imagination.

You're almost ready to start walking the path to financial greatness! You've got the motivation, the general direction, your starting point, and you know where you want to end up. You've brainstormed all the possible pitfalls you might encounter along the road and prepared for them. And here's some very good news: you're going to have a lot of help on your journey to financial greatness. Turn the page and start discovering the valuable resources you already possess that will help you get much farther much faster than you ever thought possible.

Step #6

What Are Your Available Resources?

Before you start your journey, you also need to know what resources you have available that will make your journey easier and more comfortable. If you know you're about to cross the Mojave Desert, doesn't it make sense to take water, sunscreen, a hat, and perhaps a dune buggy to help you get to the other side faster? And if you can get to the other side of the desert by plane, why walk?

In this step you're going to make a list of all the resources that might help you in your journey to financial greatness. You can divide your resources into several different categories. There are *internal* resources (beliefs, emotions, experiences from your past), and *external* resources (time, money, friends, family, information, and so on). There are also *current* resources (things or people you can access immediately) and *potential* resources (people you could find, information you could gather, money you could borrow, etc.). Remember, the path to financial greatness is a journey, not an instantaneous "thing" you acquire. The resources you have, and the resources you need, will change as you travel the path.

One of the most valuable yet underutilized resources is a role model. In the thousands of years of human history and the billions of people on this planet, there will be someone who has already achieved the goal you are seeking. In fact, there are probably many people. Your first job is to find others who already have mastered the path to your goal so you can adopt their ideas and strategies. After all, why reinvent the wheel if someone has already done it for you? Why blaze a trail if Lewis and Clark have already cleared the way?

The key to choosing a role model, however, is to *find someone who has already done it, not just someone who says they know the way.* No one can really teach what they haven't done themselves. Look at it this way. Suppose you were one of the first Europeans heading to the New World after Christopher Columbus returned to Spain in 1492. Who would you want to sail with—someone who actually went with Columbus or someone who had simply heard Columbus's stories about the voyage? Who do you think would be more likely to get you to the New World safely? Given the choice, I'd go with the person who had sailed the route himself. That's what you want in a role model. If you want to improve your relationship with your kids, find a role model who has a great relationship with his or her children. If you want to start a small business, find someone who has already established a successful enterprise. If you want advice on investing for your retirement, look at the adviser's track record and make sure he or she has done a good job over the years whether the market's up or down.

Success leaves clues, so try finding them before you start your journey. If you don't know anyone personally who has attained your goal, then read about someone who has. Be creative. Ask family and friends to help you brainstorm other potential resources. "Ask and you shall receive" is my motto! I bet there are many available resources that you have never even thought about before. But now is the time to recognize your resources and prepare to use them to the fullest on your journey.

Step 6: What Are Your Available Resources?

For each goal, answer the following questions. Write the answers on a sheet of paper or in your journal, preferably next to the appropriate goal.

▶ *What are the* external *resources available to me* right now *as I pursue this goal?*

These could include time, money, friends, family, knowledge, education, etc. List absolutely everything that could be an asset to you in pursuing this particular goal. If you want to start a pizza delivery business, do you have a car? If you want to get closer to your kids, do you know how to play video games, or can you read them stories at night? If you want to invest in a piece of property, do you have a cousin or friend or family member in real estate, banking, construction, etc.? List even the smallest resource that might be helpful.

▶ *What are the external resources available to me* in the future *as I pursue this goal?*

Assuming this goal will take you more than a month to achieve, what resources might you have access to in the future that would be helpful? Can you get a line of credit to help you grow a business? Can you take out a second mortgage on your home once you've built up the equity? Are you planning on getting a promotion or a degree that might be helpful? Will your children be graduating from college and moving away from home, thereby freeing up more money to put aside for retirement? In the same way you looked at potential obstacles in your path, you can look at potential resources that might help you. Again, be creative. There are many resources that arise that we plan for and others we do not. The key is to take advantage of as many resources as possible.

▶ *What are the* internal *resources available to me as I pursue this goal?*

What beliefs do you have about yourself that could make your journey easier? What past experiences have you had that will give you an edge? What emotions can you call on that will keep you motivated and excited? List every single belief, emotion, and experience that you could consider a resource, now and in the future.

▶ *Who might be a role model for me in pursuing this goal? Why is he or she a good role model? What can I learn from him or her that will help me in achieving this goal?*

Remember, role models can come from many different places: people you know, people you would like to know, famous people, people unknown to anyone but you, historical figures you read about in books, people you hear about on TV, etc. If possible, contact this person and see if you can sit down with him or her. If not, read about this person; learn as much as you can about how he or she achieved the goal you want to achieve. Imagine this person in your situation and ask, "What would (role model) do?" Use the person's experience and expertise to make your journey easier.

Isn't it great to realize how many resources you have at your command to help you as you walk the path to financial greatness? Now you're ready to start planning the actual steps you will need to take. You've got the *why*, you know the *what*, and you have a clear idea of what might get in your way as well as what will be of help as you walk the path. Finally, you're ready to see *how* you will get from point A (where you are) to point B (your goal). Turn the page and start planning your strategy for success.

Step #7

What's Your Strategy?

ongratulations! You've finally gotten to the *how* part. This is where you start to develop a plan of action, to build your road map to financial greatness. And it's completely up to you how you want to get there. Do you want to take the scenic route or the most direct route? Would you prefer to stop and smell the roses or do you want to take the carpool lane? Are you going to hire a personal guide or are you going to do it alone?

Some people are in a hurry to reach financial greatness, and they want to hop right into the car and start speeding off. That's fine, as long as they have a road map. Without one, they're just driving with no sense of which road will get them to their destination in the fastest, most direct way. Without a map, all they're doing is wasting gas. If you think I'm exaggerating, how many times have you heard someone say, "I need to start saving for my kids' education," but when you ask them, "How are you going to do it? What's your strategy?" they have no idea? Or they want to put aside as much money as possible for retirement, but their retirement funds are in 3 IRAs, 10 different mutual funds, plus a savings account that pays almost no interest? That's like getting into a car and starting to drive without a clear road map. To reach financial greatness, you've got to have a plan—a strategy.

What is a strategy? It's a specific way for getting from point A, where you are now, to point B, where you want to go—your goal. If your goal is to buy a house, for example, you'd better start by figuring out everything you will need to do to make that happen. Will you need to save for a down payment? Apply for a mortgage? Find a neighborhood you'd like to buy a house in? Choose a realtor? All these tasks will be part of the "road map" to your goal of owning a house.

Your strategy for reaching financial greatness will depend upon three factors: where you want to go (the goals you chose in Step 4); where you're starting from (which you discovered in Step 3); and how long you plan the trip will take. If you are saving for retirement and you're in your twenties, you might choose very different strategies than when you're in your forties. If you're saving for your child's education and he's already 16, you'd better plan a quick trip!

If your goals are going to take you several years to attain, you might want to make sure your strategy includes what I call a few rest stops. By that I mean you might want to break your goals down into smaller pieces, so you can experience the feelings of success and accomplishment of achieving something that's important to you. If you're saving for the down payment on a house, for instance, and you know it's going to take you 5 years to do so, let yourself celebrate when you get halfway to your goal. On the other hand, if your goal is to give your daughter a wonderful wedding and you know she's getting married in a year, that's a short enough trip that you won't even need to pack a lunch.

Now, there are some roads that are more heavily traveled than others, right? Here in Los Angeles, freeways like the 405 and Interstate 10 are filled with hundreds of thousands of commuters every day. These routes are busy because, for many people, they are the best roads to get from point A to point B—from home to work, for instance. In the same way, there are certain routes to financial greatness that almost everyone has to travel. These routes are the 11 different financial strategies I'm going to describe in this chapter. These simple, practical financial strategies are time-tested and proven to work. I suggest you review each one and implement as many as possible.

11 Basic Financial Planning Strategies

▶ **Get clear about your ideal outcome.**
As I discussed in the previous chapters, clarity is power. Know what truly matters most. Don't waste your time chasing after goals that really don't matter and won't create greatness in your life. That's why Steps 1, 2, and 3 of this financial greatness process are essential. Don't proceed any further until you have discovered your important life focus areas, values, roles, and goals.

▶ **Know your starting point.**
Once you get clear about your ideal outcome for your journey, you need to know where you are starting. You should have

already done some of this as part of Step 4. The key to knowing your starting point is to *get organized*. Most people don't even know or understand the assets they already possess, or the different kinds of debts they owe. Gather all your financial documents: your bank statements; investment statements, including IRAs, 401(k)s, and so on; insurance policies; most recent pay stub; last year's tax return; and employer benefit statements. Review them and make sure you know what you have.

► **Track your expenses.**
You need to track where and what you are spending your money on. This helps you analyze if you are spending too much money on things that you don't need and that are keeping you from attaining financial greatness. It also will tell you how much discretionary income you have left each month to put toward your goals. Creating and sticking to a budget ensures that you put your money where it truly matters, instead of ending the month with nothing to show for it.

► **Prepare a net worth statement.**
Most people think if they earn more money, then they will be wealthier. Nothing is farther from the truth. The more money you make, the more money you spend. We have all heard a thousand times that it is not what you earn but what you keep. Financial greatness is all about equity, not income. A net worth statement is a list of the dollar value of what you own and what you owe. The difference tracks your wealth. This is the best tool to see if you are on the right path to your journey to financial greatness. A negative net worth (more debt than assets) that is growing worse tells you that you are going the wrong

way. An increasing positive net worth means you are getting closer.

By the way, buying and owning a home is almost always the most significant part of anyone's net worth. Through the years, this is usually one of the best investment you can make. Home ownership eliminates the expense of rent every month (which does not help you build your net worth) and provides many tax advantages as well.

▶ **Build a cash reserve for confidence.**
You need to build a cash reserve for the unexpected emergencies in life. Lack of financial liquidity (that is, available cash) creates undue stress. Lack of cash reserves can sometimes almost feel like a form of slavery. Many Latinos would lose their homes if they suddenly found themselves out of a job with no severance pay. Many Latinos also find themselves in jobs they hate but can't quit because they have no cash reserve. They know that if they quit their lousy jobs, they may not find another one right away, and then they would lose their homes and credit.

▶ **Hope for the best but prepare for the worst.**
We don't like to think about things like being in an accident, or having our homes burn down, or even losing a spouse. Yet if we don't prepare, those kinds of major catastrophes can destroy us (and our families) unnecessarily. Review your insurance policies to make sure that you are properly covered for the major catastrophes of life. Review your health, life, disability, auto, homeowner's (or renter's), and long-term care insurance.

▶ Do "occupation planning."

As wealth is based on net worth instead of income, your income is the money stream that you will use to create your net worth and thus your wealth. Are you currently earning what you're worth? Sometimes we get too complacent about our jobs, and we end up not making career moves that might be to our advantage. In other circumstances, we might find ourselves in situations where we are being taken advantage of because we're not being paid what we are worth. Check to see if you truly are doing what you love and are getting paid according to the value you provide. Very few people ever review their earning potential when preparing a financial plan. Remember, *you* are the very best investment that you own.

▶ Save taxes through planning, not preparation.

Less than 3 percent of Latinos ever do any type of tax planning. Do you realize that you will pay more in taxes in your lifetime than you will ever pay for your home? One common way to know if you are not doing enough tax planning is to see if you are getting a large refund. Large refunds are usually nothing more than overwithheld money from your paycheck. You are giving the government too much money each month, which the government then refunds to you after April 15. However, does the government pay you interest on that money? Of course not!

To top it all off, most people then use their tax refunds to pay off credit card debt. Think about it: They pay the government too much each month in taxes and then charge stuff on their credit cards at 13 to 21 percent interest. But if they paid the right amount of taxes each month, they could use that money to buy the stuff they were charging and save themselves all those interest payments! Unfortunately, most people I have explained this to agree with me but can't get themselves to change this poor habit. Don't be a Latino who understands the truth but lives a lie. The truth will set you free!

► **Make and check your investments regularly.**

The path to financial greatness always includes some kind of investment plan. Make sure you are investing regularly, consistently, and in the best financial vehicles for your goals. But you can't just find an investment adviser, tell him or her what to do, and then assume everything is okay. No one cares for your money like you do. You're the one who is ultimately responsible for the health of your financial portfolio. You must review your investment portfolio regularly to make sure your investments are in line with your risk level, time line, and financial greatness goals. As I said in Barrier 2, diversification is the key to safety in your investments, and consistent investing is the key to building your portfolio safely.

Financial greatness means applying discipline to your investments. Many people lose their shirts trying to time the market—buy low, sell high. Even professionals have a hard time doing this, and unless you're planning to spend a lot of time (and money) learning about the stock market, don't try to time the market. Regular investment in a diverse range of financial vehicles (as we discussed in Barrier 2) is your best bet for building your portfolio. Discipline also means avoiding emotion when it comes to buying or selling any investment.

I've seen so many people burned when they held on to a losing stock because they "liked the company" or felt stupid because they made a bad decision when they bought the stock in the first place. While you want to use emotion to motivate you to achieve financial greatness, when it comes to buying or selling investments, your cold, hard, common sense is your best friend. When you check your portfolio, be ruthless. Weed out investments that aren't doing well, and buy more of those that are.

▶ **Educate yourself and your family.**

Absolutely the best investment you can make is to invest in a great education for yourself and your children. Unfortunately, a great education can be very costly. But as someone once said, if you think education is expensive, you should try ignorance. Make your children's education a priority; and make sure you are investing in keeping your own skills and education current with your profession's standards. It's the best way I know of to ensure a healthy income for yourself and your kids in the future.

And make sure you educate your children about finances, too. The best way to give them a secure financial future is to get them used to handling and managing money. Give them an allowance, but insist they set up a bank account with it. Employ them around the house and pay them a set wage for their time and effort. Play money games with them, like Monopoly. Show them how to balance a checkbook. Nowadays there are many books, games, and other teaching tools available for kids of all ages. When you teach your children about money—through education, practice, and your own example—you're starting them off right on their own journey to financial greatness.

▶ **Transfer your wealth to your loved ones efficiently and effectively.**

We obviously don't know when our number will be up, but because of this, we have to be ready now. Most Latinos mention family as their most important value, yet very few Latinos ever create any type of will or trust so they can protect their families' interests. This whole book is about living a financially great life from this point forward, day in and day out, and that includes the day we die. Give your family the best gift they can have in trying times: a legally and financially sound plan that makes your wishes clear and that transfers the greatest amount of your wealth to them.

How do you create your own personalized strategies? You begin by writing down all the detailed tasks you will need to do in order to achieve your goals. These detailed tasks are your action steps. Some of these steps you can do alone, others will be easier if you hire a guide (a financial professional) or buy a map (a book on tax planning, a software program, etc.). To be successful, however, make sure you devise strategies that are simple and practical. One of the secrets of financial greatness is to uncomplicate your life, not to introduce more complexity. Simplicity is the best course of action.

"*Saber es poder,*" is a motivational saying often used among Latinos. It means knowledge is power. But I firmly believe that knowledge is only *potential* power. You can have all the knowledge in the world, but if you never apply it, it won't have any impact in your life. Thinking determines what you want, but action determines what you get. When you come up with strategies, you are creating a plan to go from thinking to creating through the means of taking action. You are literally creating the means to turn your goals and dreams into your daily experience of life.

Step 7: What's Your Strategy?

For each goal, answer the following questions. Write the answers on a sheet of paper or in your journal, preferably next to the appropriate goal.

▶ *What actions do I need to take to accomplish this goal?*
Be very specific when you create your strategy. Remember to take into account three factors: where you want to go (the goal); where you're starting from (which you discovered in Step 3); and how long you plan the trip will take.

▶ *Do any of these actions require an "action plan" of their own?*
Some actions require more than one step or strategy to accomplish them. For example, suppose your strategy is to save a certain amount of money each month for the next three years to put toward starting a new business. You could do that by earning more money, cutting expenses, or a combination of the two. Some sort of plan will be required to accomplish these actions. Take a look at your actions and see how many strategies it will take to accomplish that particular step in the path to your goal.

▶ *Which of the 11 basic financial planning strategies listed in this chapter do I need to implement in my life right now?*
Have you already created strategies for some of these actions? If you have, evaluate those strategies. If you haven't handled any particular area, create that action plan now.

Strategies give us the road map to our own personal financial greatness. But there's something else that will make your journey even easier, something that will make your progress automatic: creating systems for implementing your strategies. Turn the page and be ready to rev your financial engines!

Step #8

What Practical Systems Must You Set in Place?

Have you ever driven a car with a manual transmission? When you do, you have to put a certain amount of focus on shifting gears, using the clutch pedal, being in the right gear for the right speed, and so on. But when you drive a car with an automatic transmission, that's all taken care of for you. You just step on the gas and the gears automatically shift depending on how fast the car is going. You don't have to think about shifting; all you have to do is use the accelerator and brake.

That's exactly what systems do for you: they make it easier for you to drive your "financial" car by making things automatic. You don't have to think about saving a certain amount from each paycheck because you set up an automatic withdrawal plan, for instance. You don't have to take the time each month to select exactly the right investments because you consulted a good financial planner and created a plan for building a diversified portfolio. Now every time you put money into your investment account, you know a certain percentage goes into cash, another percentage goes into mutual funds, some goes into T-bills, and so on. You also have a system in place to review your portfolio every quarter to make sure your investment goals are being met. If strategies are the road map to financial greatness, systems make your journey faster, smoother, and easier.

I once heard, "To make something powerful you need to make it practical." Systems help us make our strategies practical. Very few people can rely on self-discipline to attain their goals. They need to implement simple systems in their life to keep them going in good or bad times. Systems allow you to put your journey on automatic pilot or cruise control. I don't know of a better way of reaching your journey to financial greatness than the implementation of simple, practical systems.

Each of the strategies you devise to help you reach your goals should also have some sort of system, an automatic way to implement that strategy. At the end of this chapter you'll go through the strategies you came up with in Step 7, and create systems for making those strategies easy. But first, wouldn't it be helpful to come up with systems for accomplishing the 11 basic financial planning strategies you learned about in the last chapter?

11 Basic Financial Planning Strategies

▶ **Get clear about your ideal outcome.**

Strategy: Discover your important life focus areas, values, roles, and goals.

System: Schedule a day right now on your calendar when you can write down your ideal goals. Don't allow anyone to interrupt you; if necessary, rent a room or go off to a secluded spot where you will have no distractions. Create urgency for this most important day. Make it a mandatory holiday. Call it your personal Financial Greatness Day. Then schedule a day at least once a year to review your areas, roles, goals, and finances.

► **Know your starting point.**

Strategy: Get organized. Gather all your financial documents: your bank statements; investment statements, including IRAs, 401(k)s, and so on; insurance policies; most recent pay stub; last year's tax return; and employer benefit statements. Review them and make sure you know what you have.

System: (1) Purchase a financial organizer to put all your most important financial information in one place. Make it a rule always to put your financial information in that one location. (2) Schedule an appointment to meet with a professional financial adviser to explain anything you don't understand or need more clarity on.

► **Track your expenses.**

Strategy: Make a budget. Keep track of where and what you are spending your money on.

System: Enter your expenses each week into some kind of record. I suggest you use a financial budgeting computer program like Quicken. If you don't have a computer, paper and pencil will be just fine. I have also included a budget worksheet in the Appendix. If done properly, you can't imagine how an expense report or budget will open your eyes to money spent unwisely. It will show you where you can cut corners and help you focus on reallocating money from things that don't matter to things that matter most.

▶ **Prepare a net worth statement.**

Strategy: Create a net worth statement based on your current assets and liabilities.

System: Use the records you organized in strategy 2 to create an annual net worth statement, preferably on the day you set aside to review your finances (see strategy 1). I have given you a copy of a net worth statement in Part 3. One caution: make sure that when you figure your net worth you haven't overestimated the value of your assets and underestimated the value of your liabilities. My experience is that almost everyone overestimates the value of the home, jewelry, and furniture that they own. Be honest, not optimistic.

▶ **Build a cash reserve for confidence.**

Strategy: Build a cash reserve for the unexpected emergencies in life.

System: The best way to build a cash reserve is to pay yourself first every paycheck. Take a portion of what you earn and pay yourself first, before you put money toward bills, expenses, and so on. While this may sound difficult, I think you'll find somehow you'll manage without it—and when you see the "emergency cash" account growing each month, you'll experience a lot more peace of mind.

Put the money in a cash account such as a savings account, money market account, money market fund, or short-term bank certificate of deposit (CD). You need to understand that this money is not to be touched except in an emergency, like losing a job, unexpected medical expenses, and so on. Knowing you can cover these kinds of expenses will help you live a more confident and financially great life.

► **Hope for the best but prepare for the worst.**

Strategy: Review your health, life, disability, auto, homeowner's (or renter's), and long-term care insurance to make sure that you are properly covered for the major catastrophes of life.

System: Schedule an appointment to review all your policies with an insurance professional. Have the insurance professional coordinate all your policies to make sure you are buying the best insurance at the most affordable price. Notice I said "affordable," not "cheapest." Often cheap insurance comes with a very high price in terms of poor coverage, lousy service, and unfulfilled promises. Focus on quality insurance companies. After all, you want to make sure your insurers will be there when and if you need them.

► **Do "occupation planning."**

Strategy: Evaluate your current job to make sure you are earning what you're worth and have good income growth potential.

System: Research your employment field so you know what other people in the same job are earning. If you're being paid less than the average wage for your field, put together a proposal for a raise. Include your accomplishments in the job and what you intend to accomplish in the future. Make your case in a clear, dispassionate manner. If you are turned down, evaluate the reasons given, and if you feel they are valid (for example, you've only been doing the job for a short while), make your case a little while down the line. If you feel the reasons aren't valid, you may wish to start looking for another job with a different company.

In fact, I believe we should all have a system in place so we can apply for another job at a moment's notice. You never know when opportunity will come knocking—or when a downturn in the economy might cause your job to vanish! Keep your resume up to date, and think about sending it out every now and then to test the job market. You can also see a professional career consultant to discuss other employment opportunities or simply to get an idea of what else is out there.

No matter what, make sure that your systems include ongoing training and skills improvement. Review what you need to do to get to the next level in your career or profession. Do you need to get more education or training? A degree or certificate? Is there another computer, financial, or business skill that would make you more valuable in your current job? Once you get any training, make sure your employer knows about it—and definitely use it to ask for a raise in your next performance review!

▶ **Save taxes through planning, not preparation.**

Strategy: Evaluate what you are currently paying in taxes to ensure you are keeping as much money as possible.

System: You might want to have your taxes prepared by a qualified professional. Look for one who does taxes for a living, and who can make recommendations for reducing your taxes by maximizing your deductions. However, remember the old saying: "If it looks too good to be true, it probably is." Make sure your adviser is getting you only legal deductions, not ones that are marginal.

If you don't want to use a professional preparer, I suggest you buy one of the good tax preparation software packages that will walk you through every legal deduction. If you don't own a computer, there are many good tax preparation guides that will also help you understand the kinds of deductions you can take.

One final word about taxes: once you've lowered your taxes to the point where you no longer get that refund, take the additional money and invest it instead of spending it. That way, you're gaining a double benefit from your systems!

▶ **Make and check your investments regularly.**

Strategy: Invest regularly, diversify, and check your investments at scheduled points in time to evaluate their returns.

System: A powerful and practical system for attaining financial freedom is having the maximum allowed pension deduction taken from your paycheck every pay period. This simple system makes it easy for you to pay yourself first after every paycheck and allows you to eventually attain financial freedom.

Another great system for investing is *dollar-cost averaging.* This is where you invest a specific amount every single month no matter what. Say you wanted to put $50 a month in a particular stock mutual fund. The cost per share of that mutual fund goes up and down depending on the stock market. Let's say this particular mutual fund ranges between $25 and $40 a share on average. Some months, your $50 will buy you 2 shares at $25 each. Some months, your $50 will buy you 1¼ shares at $40 each. But over the course of a year, your average cost per share will be somewhere above $25 and below $40. With dollar-cost-average investing, you usually end up paying less than you would if you had bought shares only when you thought they were a good deal. Dollar-cost averaging is also a great way of investing consistently—which is what we want to do, right?

Once you've created systems for regular investing, you also need a system to check on your investments from time to time. Schedule a time each quarter to review your investments to make sure they are in line with your risk tolerance, time line, and financial greatness goals. Remember, diversification is the key.

Finally, when you're starting an investment program, choose a financial professional who will discuss what is important to you, figure out how much risk you are willing to take, and help you invest your way to financial greatness. This is a surefire way to know if an investment professional is on the up and up. But run as fast as you can from financial planners who are really investment salespeople. These are the ones who claim they know the next hot investment or try to sell you stocks based on prior performance. *Prior investment returns are no indication of future returns.* No one, absolutely no one, can consistently guess what the stock market is going to do in the future. If someone says she can, walk out of her office and find an honest financial adviser who will give you expert advice based on your goals.

► **Educate yourself and your family.**
Strategy: Set aside regular sums of money to invest in education for yourself and your children.
System: There are many tax-efficient ways to save for education. See a financial professional who also specializes in taxes to explain the ideal ways to save for college. For yourself, ongoing professional education is usually a tax-deductible expense. Your financial professional can help you assess what's deductible and what isn't.

► **Transfer your wealth to your loved ones efficiently and effectively.**
Strategy: Create a legally and financially sound plan that makes your wishes clear, and that transfers the greatest amount of your wealth to your family when you pass on.
System: My word of advice here is to see an estate planning attorney. (Do *not* see a *notario* if you are living in the United States. In the United States *notarios* are not attorneys like they are in most Latin American countries.) Depending on your situation, preparing a simple will or trust doesn't have to cost a lot of money, but it can save your family thousands when the time comes. However, make sure your attorney specializes in estate law. Why? Most times it is worse to prepare a bad will or trust than not to prepare one. I tell my clients that if you prepare a bad tax return you can still amend it, but you can't

amend a bad will or trust once you die. See a qualified professional from the beginning. Don't you think your family is worth it?

Your strategies are the thinking part of how to do something; the systems are your implementation. Knowledge plus action equals wisdom, and wisdom is the implementation of strategies and systems. Strategies and systems together create elegant solutions for attaining your ideal outcomes in the journey to financial greatness.

Step 8: What Practical Systems Must You Set in Place?

For each goal, answer the following questions. Write the answers on a sheet of paper or in your journal, preferably next to the appropriate goal.

▶ *For each of the strategies I created in Step 7, what systems can I set in place that will make it easier to achieve my goals?*

Remember, a good system makes progress toward your goal automatic; you don't even have to think about it anymore. Make sure your systems are very practical. With some systems, it may take a little effort to put them in place, but once they are implemented, they should be relatively effortless.

▶ *Which of the systems for the 11 basic financial planning strategies listed in this chapter do I need to implement in my life right now?*

Feel free to adopt any of the systems or strategies listed in this chapter. I've seen how effective they are for scores of my clients, and I believe they'll work for you, too.

You now know exactly where you're going and how to get there (strategies), and you've created plans for a "car" (systems) that will get you to your destination in style. Now it's time to hit the road. Before moving on to Step 9, you need to start *taking action*. Implement as many of your strategies and systems as you can in the next two weeks. The key to success is consistent action. Follow the road map you've created. Don't let yourself be tempted by side trips: keep your eyes focused on your eventual goals.

And keep your "car" filled with the fuel of motivation produced by your life focus areas, roles, and values. Why do you want to achieve these goals? Because they are important to you as a father, a spouse, an entrepreneur. Because you value family, or spirituality, or success. How much easier is it to invest instead of spending that $25 when you know it's going to buy you a house in 5 years or put your daughter through college? Look at your areas, roles, values, and goals at least once a day to keep you excited and motivated.

Now, like most road trips, it's important to keep track of where you've gotten to on the road, so you'll know how much farther you have to go to reach your destination. That's what Step 9 is all about: checking your progress as you go. By the way, congratulations on the progress you've made in this book. You're almost there—your plan to create financial greatness is in place, and you're on the road.

Step #9

Monitor Your Progress Along the Way

Imagine you're taking a trip with your family one weekend. You're going to visit your sister Lupe, who lives about 5 hours away by car. You pack your bags, fill the car with gas, get a good map, and then set off bright and early Saturday morning. You know where you want to go, you have a pretty good idea which road you'll be taking, and you know about how much time you should allow to get to Lupe's (depending on traffic). As you're on the road, you compare how far you've traveled with the amount of time you thought it would take you to get to that point. It took you an hour to go 50 miles, for example. Or perhaps you ran into a traffic jam, and you're not quite as far as you thought you would be. It's going to take you longer to get to Lupe's than you anticipated, so you pull off the road and give Lupe a call to let her know that you'll be late. Or perhaps you try a new route that shaves 15 miles off the length of the drive, allowing you to reach the halfway point of your trip much faster. But all along the way, you're monitoring your progress from your house to Lupe's. You're assessing how far you've come, how far you still have to go, and how long the trip is taking.

That's what Step 9 is all about: monitoring your progress along the road to financial greatness. Especially when it comes to finances, consistent measuring and monitoring are critical skills for assessing the journey. It's like having one of those computers in your car that keeps track of your gas mileage. You know how much power you're getting for the money (the fuel) you're putting into your financial "car," and how much more you'll need to get to your final destination.

When you monitor your financial progress, you're assessing how well what you are doing is working. You do this by asking yourself two fundamental questions: "Where am I now?" and "Where is this in relation to my ideal goal or outcome?" If you're not making the kind of progress you thought you would be, you need to make some adjustments. If you're not saving as much per month toward your house down payment, for instance, then you need to see how you can change what you're currently doing. Can you cut expenses more? Get a second job? Maybe investigate a bigger loan or see if you can get the house you want even if your down payment is smaller?

Monitoring your progress frequently is critical, because if you wait too long you might end up way off course, with valuable time and energy lost. If you've ever taken a trip in an airplane, you've benefited from the pilot's frequent monitoring of the progress the plane is making. If he or she failed to check the progress of the plane frequently, making small adjustments to keep the plane on course, you could end up hundreds of miles away from where you were supposed to land! You don't want to waste time and energy getting yourself back on track on the "flight" to financial greatness. You need to keep checking your own progress on a regular basis, to make sure your own flight is on track.

What's the best way to monitor your progress? *Establish in advance specific benchmarks to evaluate if you are on the right course.* Think of it as grade levels in school or the steps in building a house. If we didn't have first, second, third, fourth grade, and so on, it would be much harder to evaluate our kids' progress, wouldn't it? But with grade levels, we can put age-appropriate materials together and teach kids in an organized way. We can also tell how well kids are learning the materials in each grade. In building a house, if we didn't have specific tasks that need to be accomplished in a certain order, we might never get the job done. But we know we have to build the foundation by a certain date so we can put in the flooring, then set up the frame for the walls, then install the wiring, then put up sheetrock, and so on. A good builder knows these benchmarks and sets the dates for their accomplishment in advance, and then checks the job's progress at regular intervals.

A couple of examples of specific financial benchmarks are:

1. A certain percentage of money saved to money earned. For example, your goal may be to save 10 percent of your income. That's your benchmark. So each month you can check to see if you have put aside 10 percent of that month's income.

2. A specific number of assets invested by a specific date. For example, "By the time I am 50 years old, I will have $150,000." With this one, you would have to create a *series* of benchmarks that would lead you to accumulate

that much by that date. You'd have to be very clear as to how much you will have to invest each year in order to have $150,000 by the time you're 50. It's like the pilot correcting the course of the plane: it's more efficient and effective to measure frequently and make a lot of small corrections early than to wait and have to make a big correction later in the flight. In the same way, if you measure how much you've invested on a yearly (or even quarterly) basis, you can make small adjustments that will help you reach your goal of $150,000 more easily and efficiently.

If by any chance you find that you are off course in your journey to financial greatness, there are several remedies. First, go back and review the strategies and systems you created in Steps 7 and 8. It could be there are better ways to reach your goals. Second, have someone help you determine if what you are doing is on target. In this case, I strongly suggest you get a second opinion from a professional guide. Don't ask advice from people who have never been there—no one can teach you what they haven't done themselves. Also, remember that you get what you pay for. If you want financial greatness, seek the advice of someone who makes his living helping people to reach their financial goals. Consulting a financial professional is like talking to a professional airline pilot: the amount of knowledge he or she has, based on many hours of flying time, is enormous. If you want to learn to fly financially, go with the pros. They'll have ideas for strategies and systems you never knew about.

If you change your strategies and systems yet still aren't getting the results you want, it may be due to motivation. Go back and review your major life focus areas, roles, and values to see if the goal you have chosen is truly as important to you now as when you first made it a priority. *If the "why" is not big enough, then you will never find the "how" to achieve your goal.* How could you? Your reasons won't be compelling enough to create the energy that will be needed to reach the end of your journey.

In truth, the best way to monitor your progress on your journey to financial greatness is with *internal* benchmarks. When you measure your efforts regularly, you'll find yourself experiencing certain feelings. These internal guideposts include:

- Peace of mind
- A sense of calmness
- A feeling of happiness
- Reduced levels of stress
- Deeper and more committed relationships with loved ones
- More balance and integrity in your life

Pretty wonderful rewards for your efforts, aren't they? And the more you monitor, the easier it is for you to experience these feelings regularly.

Be aware, however, that the journey to financial greatness isn't something that's accomplished in a week, month, or year, so you can't measure every day and expect to see big results. When you were young, did you ever measure your height to see how much you'd grown? Maybe you were so eager that you asked your parents to measure you every day (maybe every hour) to see if you'd grown any taller since the last time. If you measured that often, would you notice a difference? Probably not. But if you waited a month or three months, you'd almost certainly notice some kind of change. Financial growth, like the growth of a child, is often a gradual process. But if you measure it on a regular basis, you'll see just how much growth is possible in what seems like a relatively short time.

Step 9: Monitor Your Progress Along the Way

For each goal, answer the following questions. Write the answers on a sheet of paper or in your journal, preferably next to the appropriate goal.

▶ *What specific benchmarks do I need to set to help me make regular progress toward this goal?*
Benchmarks could include (1) a specific amount of money set aside, (2) a specific percentage of income saved, (3) specific actions taken (choosing a financial professional, for example, or opening an investment account, or setting up an automatic withdrawal pension investment at your job). Decide what benchmarks you need to set that will help you evaluate your progress toward this particular goal.

▶ *When will I assess my progress? How frequently will I check in?*
This will depend on the benchmarks you have chosen. If you get paid every week, you might want to check in weekly. If your benchmarks have to do with specific actions, set a reasonable amount of time to accomplish what you have said you will do. However, I recommend that amount of time is no longer than 1 month to 3 months. If you check in less than four times a year on a goal, you run the risk of getting way off course by the time you get around to noticing.

When it comes time to monitor your progress based on the specific benchmarks you have chosen, ask yourself the following questions.

▶ *Where am I now? Is this where I said I would be in my progress toward this goal?*
Be honest. This is not the time for excuses or reasons why you have or haven't accomplished what you said you would do. Just make the clearest, cleanest possible evaluation of where you are in relation to where you said you would be.

▶ *What do I need to do more/differently/less in order to achieve the progress I want?*

If you've achieved your benchmark, congratulations! You might want to take a look at what you're doing and see if there's a way you can get even better results even faster. If you've missed your target, now's not a time to beat yourself up. That isn't helpful. However, it is a time to evaluate what you're doing, figure out what's not working, and change your approach. First, look at your motivation. Go back and review your major life focus areas, roles, and values to see if the goal you have chosen is truly as important to you now as when you first made it a priority. If not, either change the goal or get more excited about what this goal will mean for you in your life. Second, look at your strategies and systems to see if there's anything you can change, improve, or eliminate. If so, you may wish to consult a financial professional for help in devising more effective strategies and systems that will help you achieve your goals.

I believe that if you're following the steps in this process and taking consistent action, you'll find monitoring your progress is a joyous step. You'll get to see how well what you're doing is working. You can also make corrections early, when it's easy to do so. And you'll get a chance to connect emotionally with the value of your progress, both in your life and the lives of your family. You'll be ready for the last step in your journey to financial greatness.

Step #10

Celebrate and Share Your Success!

This last step will not only keep you on the right path but also will definitely help you keep from getting lost as you travel through life. Have you ever not known where to turn next? Have you achieved a goal and wondered what was next? How did you feel? Most people live their lives anxious, frustrated, worried, and stressed out. These negative emotions cause tremendous pain, especially if they're accompanied by a sense that we're living lives without purpose. But when you're following the 10 steps—when you know what's important to you and why it's important, when you have clear strategies and systems and you monitor your progress—you stand a much better chance of living a life that is full of meaning, one you can be proud of when you reach your final destination.

Step 10 is one of the most important steps in the entire process, yet it's one that all too often we forget or ignore. We get so caught up in the journey that we don't look up and realize we've arrived. Even when we've made it, we don't make a big deal out of our accomplishment because we're already working on the next goal, or the next task, or the next project. We finally save the money for the down payment, for instance, but now we're focused on the process of buying the house. We put the last dollar in Junior's college fund, only now we're worried about paying the next kid's tuition. In this way, we cheat ourselves out of some of the most important moments in our lives.

In truth, when we don't take the time to celebrate our successes, we sabotage our own efforts. The biggest rewards on the journey to financial greatness have nothing to do with money and everything to do with our emotions. Money is not the end, just the means—the fuel for your journey. As you recall, the first three steps of this process revolved around motivation, creating enough positive emotion to keep you moving toward your goals. Well, emotion is just as important at the end as it is in the beginning. Celebration gives you the kind of emotional reward that will cause you to want to keep pursuing your goals, whether it's this goal or another one.

Celebration is also a great way to involve the people you care about in your goals and outcomes. Many people unfortunately achieve goals in life without having anyone to share them with. As I explained in Part 1 of this book, many people reach a certain level of success yet find it to be a very lonely experience. They end up asking, "Is this all there is?" That kind of success is not financial greatness. But I believe financial greatness is meant to be shared and celebrated with the people we love. True financial greatness is knowing that you have attained all your most important goals while living with purpose and significance, surrounded by people you love and who love you. And that's a cause for celebration!

But here's the real secret to Step 10: you have to plan your celebrations in advance. That way, you'll continue to be motivated to make progress. Have you ever planned a party to celebrate a birthday, anniversary, christening, or other major life event? Isn't the anticipation and fun of planning a great part of the whole experience? Didn't the planning process make you feel happy and eager for the important day to arrive? And when the party happened, wasn't it great to be surrounded by people you loved as you celebrated? It's the same with planning your goal achievement celebration. Having that to look forward to, and the anticipation of sharing your success with the people you love, will make you even more eager to achieve financial greatness.

Another great motivator in the journey to financial greatness is not to wait until the end to celebrate, but to have minicelebrations along the way. Remember those benchmarks you set for yourself in Step 9? Why not celebrate when you reach them? When you achieve your goal of setting aside 10 percent of your income for the month, for instance, treat yourself and your kids to something special. When you meet your goals in terms of saving a certain amount toward retirement, have a "preretirement" party. Even simple rewards and celebrations, like cards, outings, an afternoon at the beach or in the woods, and so on, can help keep you motivated to achieve and do more toward your goals.

For some goals it's a little more difficult to declare, "Yes! I've made it! I've achieved what I set out to do!" Financial goals are sometimes easy to measure, but what about relationship goals? For example, when will you know you've achieved a great relationship with your spouse or your kids? That's why it's so important to be very, very specific in Step 4 when you create your goals. If other people are involved in your goals, you might want to get their agreement about what that goal will look and feel like once you've achieved it. How will your spouse know that your relationship is better? How will your kids know you're a better parent? Then you can monitor your progress in this goal (Step 9), set benchmarks, and be ready to celebrate when the time comes! (In fact, Step 4 is also a great time to plan the celebration you'll have in Step 10.)

Last, and most important: *Never* move on to a new goal in this area until you have celebrated the goal you have just achieved. If your goal was to get a better job, have a party before you start the new one. If your goal was to lose 20 pounds, do something to celebrate before you tackle losing another 10. You've got to reward yourself emotionally for your achievements because emotional rewards are what we're truly after. When you give yourself the chance to ring the bell, to pat yourself on the back, and, most important, to share your success and joy with the people you love, then you'll not only enjoy the destination but you'll enjoy the process of getting there.

Someone once said, "Anticipation is the best sauce for a meal." The anticipation of celebration is the best reward I know of to make the journey to financial greatness more pleasurable every step of the way.

EXERCISE

Step 10: Celebrate and Share Your Success!

For each goal, answer the following questions. Write the answers on a sheet of paper or in your journal, preferably next to the appropriate goal.

▶ *How will I celebrate my success when I achieve this goal?*
Make sure your celebration is something you will truly enjoy and can look forward to with pleasure. Do you want to throw a party? Give yourself something special? Send out an announcement? Take a vacation or a break? Whatever your celebration, make sure it has meaning for you.

▶ *Who do I want to include in my celebration?*
Sharing a celebration with those we love makes it truly special. You might want to invite those who helped you with this particular goal, or just those whose lives have touched you along the way.

▶ *What minicelebrations can I plan when I hit some of the benchmarks I set up in Step 9?*
Make sure every celebration makes you feel really great about your efforts to date while keeping you motivated to continue your progress toward your ultimate goal.

Congratulations! You have accomplished something remarkable. You have taken what was once a dream and turned it into a tangible reality. You are among the very few in this world who take action instead of wasting time in excuses. You have blazed a trail to the ultimate destination of financial greatness—an "El Dorado" that contains not just financial abundance, but abundance in every important area of life. You are ready for the last, most important secret, the one that will help you expand beyond your current success. Turn the page to discover the ultimate secret!

Financial Greatness Is Just the Beginning

Do you remember the steps in the road to financial greatness? Survival, struggle, stability, success, and finally financial greatness? Well, even though everyone travels on similar "roads," I hope you've figured out by now that everyone's version of financial greatness will be a little bit different, depending on the roles, values, and goals he or she has. I may feel I have arrived when I have a nice house in a good neighborhood, a solid marriage, enough money in the bank to put my kids through college and to provide for retirement. For my cousin Carmen, it might be a business worth $3 million, a big house and a vacation home, and trips to Europe two times a year. For others, it might be good health care, a secure retirement income, and being able to treat their grandkids to ice cream every once in a while. Everyone is different—but somehow, we all have a sense when we've arrived at the place we call financial greatness.

Remember our original definition: Financial greatness is an abundance of love, confidence, and money. It's having the courage to live the life of your dreams, knowing that your life matters. Ultimately, it's a mindset based on a clear vision of who you want to become. Throughout this book, I have taken you through a process designed to create the mindset of financial greatness. Once you develop the mindset, then taking the actions to create that abundance of love, confidence, and money becomes easy. You know where you want to go, why you wish to do so, and how to get there. Then it's just a matter of effort through time to make your dreams of financial greatness your daily reality.

But how do we know when we have arrived at our destination? When we take a trip somewhere we usually know when we have arrived because there is a signpost telling us so. What are the signs you will receive when you arrive at your own financial greatness?

Here's the secret: The truest signs will not be external signs, like a big house, a successful business, or money in the bank. Your truest signs will be internal; they will be how you feel about yourself and your life. Besides seeing an abundance of wealth, you will know you have arrived when you feel profound peace of mind, happiness, joy, abundance, and confidence. You know when you have arrived when you don't feel envy, jealousy, guilt, and fear. These internal signs are the best indicators to let you know that you have arrived at the place of financial greatness. Because ultimately financial greatness has far less to do with what you have and far more to do with who you have become.

I have met many people who have lots of money and live miserable lives, and many poor people who live happy lives. Misery and happiness have very little to do with money; but they have a great deal to do with how rich we are in fulfillment. A financially great life is one that allows you to live your ideal life, the one you just mapped out through the course of this book. When you know you are living the life you designed, one in which you are pursuing the dreams that have meaning for you and those you love, then you will know you are truly happy.

It's Your Life—It's Your Choice

Imagine it's a beautiful spring day, and you're going somewhere special. You walk into a tastefully decorated room, with thick carpet and plush drapes. Soft music is playing in the background. You look around and you see that all the people who know and love you are here, too. Then you notice a large wooden rectangular box against one wall of this room. It's a coffin. You walk toward the box and look inside—and see yourself! You're at your own funeral. Everyone sits down, and then one by one, the people who were closest to you stand up and talk about you. They are completely honest; they talk about your good and bad points. They share every detail of your life, including how they felt about you. What would they say? If your funeral were held tomorrow, how would people describe your life so far? If it happened 20 years in the future, how would you like them to talk about your life: your accomplishments, your relationships, how you were viewed, what you contributed?

This mental exercise is a great reminder of the final destination for us all. No matter what road we take—whether we make it to financial greatness or stay in the swamp of struggle and survival—we all end up at the same point. What truly matters is what we do with our lives before those eulogies are delivered. And that is completely and utterly up to us. The only way to travel the road to greatness, financial or otherwise, is to realize that *we* are in control, that we have to decide how we're going to live each day and then live it as best we can, according to the design we have created for ourselves. We can't let circumstances dictate our dreams or hinder our efforts. There's an old saying, *"Cada quien contruye su propio destino."* Each person builds his or her own destiny. When you know you are living a life in which you are following your dreams, and those dreams make life better not only for you but also for those you love, your community, and perhaps even the world as a whole, then somehow the end of the road looks a whole lot brighter. Your eulogy will be filled with love and appreciation for a life of greatness that made a difference. And you can look on with pride and great peace of mind, knowing the world is better for your having spent time on it.

But the end is determined by each choice we make along the way. And it also depends on our constantly and consistently achieving our goals and setting new ones. In truth, financial greatness isn't really a destination. It's a process. We don't reach greatness—we become great. And when we are great, we know that every goal contains within it the seeds of an even greater dream. The secret of greatness is always to raise the bar, for ourselves and for what we believe we can achieve. I'm not saying you should never be satisfied; you've got to enjoy what you accomplish or you'll never want to achieve even more. But those who understand true greatness know how to celebrate and enjoy their success even as they look forward to the next step up.

That's the real secret for a great life: The truly happy people have figured out how to enjoy the journey. So that's my final request to you. I hope you will take on these 10 steps and use them to start your own journey to financial greatness. But more than that, I hope you will find as many ways as you can to enjoy every step, no matter how small or large, trivial or meaningful, easy or difficult, quick or slow. I challenge you to use the creativity and energy God has given each of us to turn your journey to financial greatness into a pilgrimage of discovery, laughter, and joy. When you can pursue each of your goals with excitement, when you attack even the most difficult tasks with enthusiasm, when you keep your commitments to yourself and others with a smile on your face and happiness in your heart, and yes, when you overcome those natural moments of laziness or fear or discouragement by keeping the pleasure of reaching your ultimate goal in your thoughts, then your journey will enrich you far more than any material riches you may accumulate along the way. And your success will be assured, because your external wealth will simply be a reflection of the greater treasures you have inside.

I look forward to hearing from you as you tread the road to financial greatness. As Cesar Chavez said, *"Si se puede."* And I also say to you, yes, you can!

Part Three

Checklists, Worksheets, and Resources

The Most Common Financial Mistakes Made by Latinos

While you may not find yourself making these mistakes, many Latinos fall into these common traps when it comes to making and managing money. Next to some of these mistakes you'll find a reference to the specific chapter in this book where I talk about the underlying reasons for this mistake, and some different ways for Latinos to approach our finances. Remember the saying, *"Saber es poder"* (Knowledge is power). By becoming aware of these mistakes, I hope you'll avoid them.

Latinos . . .

- Approach the wrong people for advice (Barrier 3).
- Consider price more important than competency. They look for the person who will give them the best deal (*quieren regatear*) (Barrier 8).
- Are embarrassed to ask questions because they don't want

to look like fools (*tienen vergüenza*) or just don't want to be a bother (*no quieren molestar*) (Barriers 3, 4, and 5).

- Work with cash and don't trust banks and don't use checking accounts (Barrier 2).
- Believe that making a double payment on a credit card bill next month because they missed the last month's payment will not ruin their credit (Barrier 4).
- Finance major items (autos, homes, furniture) without understanding the terms and documents they are signing (Barrier 4).
- Cosign loans for family members and friends who have bad credit (Barrier 4).
- Believe that the lottery is an investment (Barrier 8).
- Believe that if they invest in their company's 401(k), their company may someday take their money (Barrier 1).
- Believe that the "best" tax preparer is the one who gets them the biggest refund (Barrier 3).
- Believe that a tax refund is a form of savings plan (Steps 8 and 9).
- Get their family involved in multilevel marketing schemes without properly investigating the companies (Barrier 8).
- Like to take short cuts (they know all the *movidas*) (Barrier 8).
- Don't prepare a will or trust, or buy life insurance because they are afraid to discuss death. They believe that as soon as they do something about it they will die (Steps 7 and 8).

The Most Common Financial Mistakes Made by Everyone

In the last list, I gave some specific mistakes that Latinos make due to our culture, but there are lots of other mistakes that everybody makes. Again, I've put references to the places where I talk about these pitfalls. Protect your future of financial greatness by avoiding these mistakes, too.

Most people . . .

- Don't have a written financial plan (Barrier 7 and 8).
- Don't have any savings for emergencies (Steps 7 and 8).
- Buy the wrong type and amount of insurance (Steps 7 and 8).
- Buy life insurance as an investment (Barrier 3).
- Believe that making more money will make them rich (Steps 7 and 8).
- Overspend and buy things on impulse (Steps 7 and 8).

- Invest before they know what their goals are: the ready-fire-aim approach (Steps 7 and 8).
- Buy investments they don't understand (Barrier 2).
- Buy or sell investments based on emotions (Step 7).
- Believe in investment gurus (Barrier 2).
- Believe that they can time the stock market ups and downs (Step 7).
- Believe friends who have an inside tip on a stock and act on it (Barrier 8).
- Don't participate in their employer's pension plan (Barrier 1).
- Wait too long to start their pension plan (Barrier 9).
- Rarely review their investment portfolios in their pension plan (Steps 7 and 8).
- Believe in the philosophy, "It will never happen to me" (Barrier 7 and Step 7).
- Are indecisive and don't implement actions due to procrastination, fear, or ignorance (Barriers 1, 4, and 5).
- Don't establish a will or a trust (Steps 7 and 8).
- Name their minor children as beneficiaries (Steps 7 and 8).
- Are disorganized and don't know where all their important financial documents are (Steps 7 and 8).
- Focus too little or too much on money (Step 1).

This road leads to poverty and financial dependence. Don't let this be you!

The Journey to Financial Greatness Checklist

While the second part of this book outlines a 10-step guide to achieving financial greatness, you can use this checklist to make sure you have covered all the bases as you take your own journey.

Those who are (or who will become) financially great do the following. They. . . .

- Have a written financial plan based on their greatest life focus areas, roles, and values (Steps 1 to 8).
- Are organized and know where all their vital financial information is (Steps 7 and 8).
- Have a budget and live within their means (Steps 7 and 8).
- Pay themselves first every pay period (Steps 7 and 8).
- Establish and fund an emergency reserve (Steps 7 and 8).

- Pay off their personal credit cards monthly (Barrier 4).
- Review their personal credit report annually (Barrier 4).
- Purchase the right type and amount of insurance (life, health, disability, auto, homeowner's, and long-term care) (Steps 7 and 8).
- Focus on tax planning, not just on tax preparation (Steps 7 and 8).
- Understand and use their employee benefits (Barrier 1).
- Have the maximum allowed contribution automatically withdrawn from their paycheck into their retirement account (Steps 7 and 8).
- Invest according to their financial objectives and risk tolerance (Barrier 2).
- Purchase a home (Step 7).
- Save for their children's future college tuition (Steps 7 and 8).
- Get expert advice on how to take title to assets or name beneficiaries on accounts (Barrier 2, Steps 7 and 8).
- Have a will or a trust completed and funded (Steps 7 and 8).
- Review their finances (at least) annually (Steps 7 and 8).
- Complete their education (they invest in themselves) (Steps 7 and 8).
- Keep their life partner informed about their finances (Barrier 5).
- Teach their children about money (Steps 7 and 8).
- Give back to their community (Barrier 6).
- Work with professionals who are specialists in their field (Barrier 3).

- Ask questions, questions, and more questions (Barrier 3 and 4).
- Report to the appropriate agencies any misconduct from financial salespeople (Barrier 4, Part 3).
- Read, read, read (Barrier 4).

Follow this checklist as your road map for the journey to financial greatness!

When Vicks and a Warm 7-Up Just Won't Do: What to Do When You Feel You Haven't Been Dealt With Honestly

When you were sick as a little kid, how did your mom take care of you? I'll bet she put you to bed, put Vicks VapoRub on your chest, and gave you warm 7-Up and chicken soup until you felt better. It'd be nice if we got that kind of TLC as adults, wouldn't it? Especially when we feel we've been taken advantage of, cheated, or dealt with in less than an honest fashion.

While the care isn't as personal as your mother's, there are places you can go when you've got a complaint. Don't hesitate to call any or all of the appropriate agencies listed here. Make sure you have all your records in front of you so you can clearly state the business or person you have the issue with and the nature of the disagreement. You might also like to have some idea of the kind of remedy you would like (to get your money back, for instance, or to void the contract, and so on).

Remember, the people at these agencies hear many, many complaints. They aren't interested in your emotion, only the facts of the dispute. Be as clear and honest as you can, and then see what they suggest.

Here is a list of agencies you can contact with complaints:

Insurance complaints: The Department of Insurance in your state.

Real estate transaction complaints: The Department of Real Estate in your state.

Employment-related complaints: The Department of Labor and the Equal Opportunity Employment Commission (EEOC) in your state.

Any kind of complaints about businesses and your investment in them: The Securities and Exchange Commission (SEC). To report Internet investment scams, contact the Securities and Exchange Commission at enforcement@sec.gov.

Complaints about financial professionals such as stockbrokers: The National Association of Securities Dealers (NASD).

Complaints about attorneys: The Bar Association for your state.

Recommended Reading List

These are some of the books I currently recommend to my clients. You may wish to check the bookstores for more current selections.

Everyone's Money Book by Jordan E. Goodman. Dearborn Trade, 2001.
The Millionaire Next Door: The Surprising Secrets of America's Wealthy by Thomas J. Stanley and William D. Danko. Longstreet Press, 1996.
Personal Finance for Dummies by Eric Tyson. Hungry Minds, 2000.
The Richest Man in Babylon by George S. Clason. Dutton, 1988.
The Road to Wealth: A Comprehensive Guide to Your Money by Suze Orman. Riverhead Books, 2001.
Smart Couples Finish Rich by David Bach. Broadway Books, 2001.
Think and Grow Rich by Napoleon Hill. Reprint edition, Fawcett Books, 1990.

Major Life Focus Areas

Use this chart to write the major life focus areas you discovered in Step 1. Some suggestions for areas you wish to focus on include: physical, relationships, spiritual, intellectual, professional, personal growth, financial, charitable, and material. Under each area, write the roles you fill in this area. Under relationships, for example, you might have "spouse," "parent," "child," "friend," "co-worker," "employee," "boss," and so on.

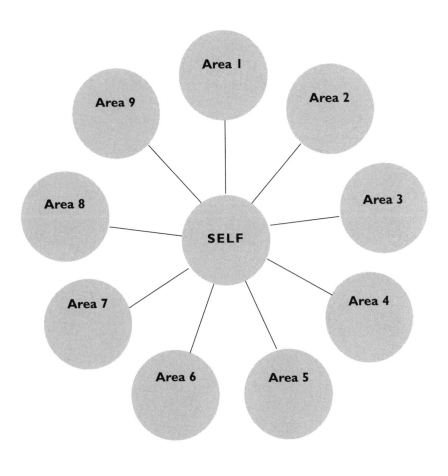

Major Life Values

For each area, write the values you consider important in this part of your life (as you discovered in Step 2). If you have a professional area, for instance, you might write values like "success," "excellence," "reliability," "courage," and so on. Under the area of finances you might have "prudence," "discernment," "education," etc.

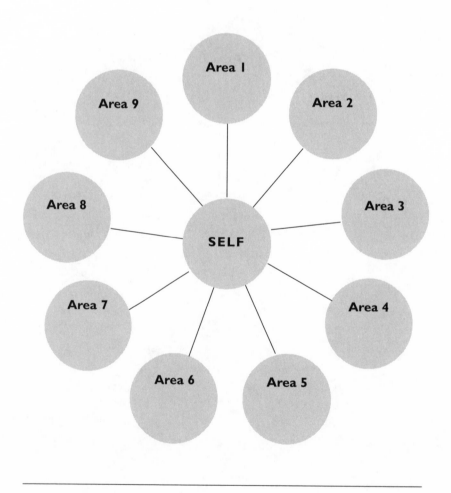

Spending Plan (Budget)

The numbers you enter should be based on what you currently spend for each of these categories. Make sure to include what is spent by you, your spouse or significant other, and your children—anyone you consider part of your household.

(See next page.)

Name: _____

Date: _____

Category	Expense	Loan Balance	Amount	Monthly Total	Annual Total
Home	Rent/Mortgage	$	$	$	$
	Mortgage (2nd or equity)	$	$	$	$
	Other Loans on Residence	$	$	$	$
	Association Dues	$	$	$	$
	Home (Renter's) Insurance	$	$	$	$
	Property Taxes	$	$	$	$
	Maintenance	$	$	$	$
	Gardener	$	$	$	$
	Housekeeper	$	$	$	$
	Household Products	$	$	$	$
	Home Furniture/Fixtures	$	$	$	$
	Home/Holiday Decorations	$	$	$	$
Utilities	Electricity	$	$	$	$
	Water	$	$	$	$
	Gas	$	$	$	$
	Waste (Trash)	$	$	$	$
	Telephone	$	$	$	$
	2nd Phone Line (Internet)	$	$	$	$
	Cell Phone/Pager	$	$	$	$

Category	Expense	Loan Balance	Amount	Monthly Total	Annual Total
Auto	Auto Loan/Lease Payment	$	$	$	$
	Auto Insurance	$	$	$	$
	Auto Registration Fees	$	$	$	$
	Gasoline	$	$	$	$
	Auto Maintenance/Repairs	$	$	$	$
	Parking	$	$	$	$
	Public Transportation	$	$	$	$
Children	Child Support	$	$	$	$
	Child Care/Babysitting	$	$	$	$
	Child Clothing	$	$	$	$
	School Support/Events	$	$	$	$
	School Tuition	$	$	$	$
	Extracurricular/Tutoring	$	$	$	$
	College Funding	$	$	$	$
Food	Groceries	$	$	$	$
	Breakfast Out	$	$	$	$
	Lunches Out	$	$	$	$
	Dinners Out	$	$	$	$
	Coffees/Smoothies/Etc.	$	$	$	$

(chart continued on next page)

Name: _____

Date: _____

Category	Expense	Loan Balance	Amount	Monthly Total	Annual Total
Clothing	Work Clothes	$	$	$	$
	Casual Clothes/Misc.	$	$	$	$
	Shoes/Accessories	$	$	$	$
	Dry Cleaning	$	$	$	$
Travel	Vacations	$	$	$	$
	Day/Weekend Trips	$	$	$	$
Entertainment	Cable TV/Movies/Rentals	$	$	$	$
	Concerts/Ball Games	$	$	$	$
	Books/Mags./Newspapers	$	$	$	$
	Music/CDs	$	$	$	$
	Hobbies	$	$	$	$
Personal	Life Insurance	$	$	$	$
	Disability Insurance	$	$	$	$
	Continuing Education	$	$	$	$
	Technology	$	$	$	$
	Postage	$	$	$	$
	Bank Service Charges/Fees	$	$	$	$
	Gym Dues/Sports Gear	$	$	$	$
	Personal Care (hair/nails/etc.)	$	$	$	$
	Entertaining/Parties	$	$	$	$

Category	Expense	Loan Balance	Amount	Monthly Total	Annual Total
Medical	Medical Insurance	$	$	$	$
	Dental Insurance	$	$	$	$
	Long-Term Care Insurance		$	$	$
	Doctor/Dentist/Optometrist	$	$	$	$
	Chiropractic/Therapist/Etc.	$	$	$	$
	Glasses/Contacts	$	$	$	$
	Prescriptions	$	$	$	$
	Insurance Deductibles	$	$	$	$
Gifts	Birthdays	$	$	$	$
	Christmas	$	$	$	$
	Anniversary/Special Events	$	$	$	$
Pets	Pet Food	$	$	$	$
	Veterinarian	$	$	$	$
	Pet—Miscellaneous	$	$	$	$
Savings	Retirement—Qualified	$	$	$	$
	Retirement—Non-Qualified	$	$	$	$
	Current Savings/Investments	$	$	$	$
Charitable	Church	$	$	$	$
	Non-Profit Organizations	$	$	$	$
	Other___	$	$	$	$

(chart continued on next page)

Name: _____

Date: _____

Category	Expense	Loan Balance	Amount	Monthly Total	Annual Total
Personal Loans	Credit Card: Visa	$	$	$	$
	Credit Card: MasterCard	$	$	$	$
	Credit Card: Amex	$	$	$	$
	Credit Card: Dept. Stores	$	$	$	$$
	Credit Card: Other_____	$	$	$	$
	School Loans	$	$	$	$
	Other Loans	$	$	$	$
Professional Fees	Accountant	$	$	$	$
	Attorney	$	$	$	$
	Financial Adviser	$	$	$	$
	Other Consultants	$	$	$	$
Taxes	Federal	$	$	$	$
	State	$	$	$	$
	SDI	$	$	$	$
	FICA	$	$	$	$
	Medicare	$	$	$	$
Miscellaneous	Alimony	$	$	$	$
	Walking Around Money	$	$	$	$

Category	Expense	Loan Balance	Amount	Monthly Total	Annual Total
Miscellaneous	Unreimbursed Employee Exp.	$	$	$	$
	Union Dues/Fees	$	$	$	$
	Miscellaneous	$	$	$	$
	Negative on Rental Properties	$	$	$	$
	Total Expenses:	$	$	$	$

Tips:

1. When an expense is annual, divide by 12 and enter.

2. If you don't know the amount, take an educated guess.

3. Review your check register for expenses.

Net Worth Statement

Name: _____

Date: _____

Assets	Amount/Current Fair Market Value
Cash	$
Savings accounts	$
Money market accounts	$
Money market funds	$
Certificates of deposit	$
Mutual funds (equity or bond)	$
Individual stocks	$
Bonds	$
Other securities	$
Notes receivable (2nd trust deeds)	$
Stock options	$
Tax-deferred annuities (nonqualified)	$
Individual retirement accounts (IRAs)	$
Roth IRAs	$
Pension plans:	$
401(k)	$
403(b) TSAs	$
457 plan	$
SEP	$
SIMPLE	$
Profit sharing (vested)	$
Other pension	$
Life insurance cash value	$
Limited partnerships	$
Personal residence	$
2nd residence (vacation home)	$
Investment property:	$
Property 1	$
Property 2	$
Property 3	$
Automobile	$

Assets	Amount/Value
Automobile	$
Boat/RV	$
Business	$
Jewelry	$
Precious metals	$
Antiques	$
Collectibles	$
Other valuable personal property	$
Other	$
Total Assets	**$**

Liabilities	Outstanding Balance	Term(s) Rate (%)	Interest	Minimum Monthly Payment
		$		$
		$		$
		$		$
		$		$
		$		$
		$		$
		$		$
		$		$
		$		$
		$		$
		$		$
		$		$
		$		$
		$		$
		$		$
Total Liabilities	**$**			**$**

———————— ———————————— ————————————

(total assets) - (total liabilities) = (current net worth)

About the Author

The son of Mexican immigrants, Louis Barajas grew up in the barrio of East Los Angeles and spent his early years helping his father by keeping the books for the family's wrought-iron business. By age 16, he was savvy enough about tax law to challenge the IRS officials who were auditing the elder Barajas. Louis argued that his father owed the government no additional money, and eventually the IRS concluded that the insistent young Barajas was right.

While attending UCLA, Louis dedicated much of his spare time to helping teenagers from his old neighborhood. He was involved in both Project Motivation and the Partnership Program, which were designed to encourage minority youths to succeed in school. After graduating with a bachelor's degree in sociology, Louis decided the best way to help his community would be through his business and financial skills. So he continued his education, receiving his MBA from Claremont Graduate School and becoming a certified financial planner and registered investment adviser. He was licensed by the Internal Revenue Service as an enrolled agent in 1991, and received a certified divorce planner designation from the Institute of Certified Divorce Planners in 1999.

While completing his graduate work, Louis accepted an excellent position at Kenneth Leventhal, a prominent accounting and consulting firm in Orange County. With offices overlooking the Newport Beach marina and millionaire clients, most young businessmen would feel they had arrived. But in 1991 Louis received a double wake-up call—the death of his beloved grandmother and the tragic suicide of his uncle. At that point Louis decided he no longer wanted the traditional definition of success; instead, he felt pulled to put his skills and abilities to work in the place he felt they were needed most—his community in East Los Angeles. In October 1991, he left his comfortable Newport Beach job and opened up a financial planning firm in the barrio.

Louis's first office was over a Mexican seafood restaurant in Boyle Heights, and clients were directed upstairs by a hand-lettered sign. He slashed his fees to 25 percent of what he had charged in Orange County and actively sought out clients who had never even heard of financial planning. Instead of consulting with millionaires, Louis was now advising grocery clerks in danger of losing their homes . . . middle-class couples who wanted parochial school education for their kids . . . immigrants who distrusted banks and saved money in Sparklett's water bottles in the kitchen . . . young men who innocently signed car loan agreements at interest rates of 25 percent . . . and many more. These were the people who needed financial planning most, but Louis found that many of them lacked the most basic information about how to make their money work harder. So he decided his most important role would be to serve as a bridge between working people and the sometimes overwhelming world of finances.

Thus, Louis Barajas & Associates expanded its services to include educating the Latino community about dealing with money. Today, its mission is to provide the finest financial planning services at reasonable rates and to educate and empower families and individuals to take control of their financial destiny and create financial greatness.

Louis is known for providing high-caliber financial planning services in a straightforward, easy-to-understand manner. Many clients want to work with him not only because of his expertise, integrity, and high ethical standards but also because of his strong and ongoing commitment to give back to the community. The offices of Louis Barajas & Associates are currently located in the Citadel, an office and shopping complex in Commerce, California. Current clients include professional athletes, professional entertainers, prominent doctors, lawyers, politicians, and business owners from all across the country.

Widely recognized for his contribution to the Latino community, Louis Barajas has been profiled in the Metro section of the *Los Angeles Times*, in *Nuestro Tiempo* and the *Wave* newspapers, in *Saludos Hispanos* magazine, the *Journal of Financial Planning*, *Research* magazine, *Assets* magazine, the *Orange County Register*, the *Tampa Tribune Times*, the *Lexington Herald-Leader*, the *Atlanta Journal*, and the *San Diego Tribune*. He makes regular appearances as a financial expert on KMEX Channel 34 Evening News and has been interviewed by Bloomberg Radio News, BIZNEWS, and many of the other news and financial radio shows in the greater Los Angeles area. Louis was selected as Financial Planner of the Month by *Mutual Funds* magazine and was featured in the CNBC special "Watch and Make Money." He is quoted regularly in *Hispanic Business* magazine. For the past five years Louis also wrote a very successful financial column for *La Opinion*, the largest Spanish-language newspaper in the United States. In September 2002, he was named as one of the top 100 planners in the country by *Mutual Funds* magazine.

Louis resides in Irvine, California with his wife, Angie, and his three children, daughters Alexa Pilar and Aubrey Marisa, and stepson Eddie.

Louis can be contacted at:
200 Citadel Drive, Suite 100
Los Angeles, CA 90040
(323) 890-8180
www.financialgreatness.com
email: louisbarajas@aol.com